DOUBLE TAKE

Two sides One story

D0639737

Rivals for the crown

MARGARET SIMPSON

SCHOLASTIC INC.

New York   Toronto   London   Auckland   Sydney
Mexico City   New Delhi   Hong Kong   Buenos Aires

This story is based, as much as possible, on primary source material — the words and pictures of the people who witnessed the events described. While it is not possible to know the exact thoughts, feelings, and motives of all the people involved, the book aims to give an insight into the experience of the events, based on the available evidence.

ISBN 0-439-69859-6

12 11 10 9 8 7 6 5 4 3 2 1   4 5 6 7 8 9/0

Printed in the U.S.A.   08

First printing, November 2004

Contents

Introduction

EVERYONE KNOWS THAT Henry VIII had six wives. The reason he kept on marrying — at least until he got to wife number three — was that he was desperate for a son to succeed him.

That son was a long time coming, but along the way Henry had two daughters, born seventeen years apart to different mothers. Henry didn't think much of women rulers, and he got into a terrible mess changing the law to keep his daughters off the throne.

This meant that both girls had a hard time — with their father *and* with each other. For whether Henry liked it or not, for a time they were his only surviving children, and this made them rivals for the crown of England. After Henry died, they were rivals again. Their brother Edward was only a boy, and if anything happened to him the Catholics wanted Mary for queen, while the "reformists" (later called Protestants) favored

Elizabeth. And so the personal rival of the Tudor sisters was also tangled up with religion, the burning issue of the day.

In the end, both princesses became queen, one after the other. One of them gained a reputation as the most successful queen England ever had; the other was loathed and reviled. Why did they turn out so differently? And how did they feel about each other? Read on to find out what life was like for the rival daughters of Henry VIII.

Mary

Beloved Only Child

1518 – 1527

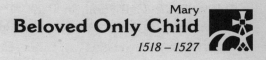

ON OCTOBER 5, 1518, King Henry VIII stood in front of his throne at the royal palace of Greenwich for an important ceremony. Beside him was his wife, Queen Catherine, and a maid of honor, who held in her arms a beautiful, blond, curly-haired toddler, just two-and-a-half years old. The toddler was the royal princess, Mary. It was the day of her betrothal to be married, and she was being promised to the baby son of the king of France. When the bridegroom reached the age of 14, Mary would be sent to him, and they would become man and wife.

In honor of the occasion, Mary wore a gold dress and a black cap studded with gold and jewels. She was known for being a good child, and she behaved herself beautifully throughout the long ceremony. As her parents consented to her future marriage, the French admiral, who was representing the king of France, pushed a ring, sparkling with a large diamond, onto Mary's chubby finger. Mary smiled.

A similar ceremony was later repeated at a high mass in Notre Dame Cathedral, in Paris. There the Earl of Worcester stood in for Mary and her parents, and the ceremony was witnessed by other English courtiers. Afterward, King Francis entertained the courtiers by taking them hunting for bears. The French court was amazingly rich, and the English were awed by its elegance and wealth. A courtyard had been specially prepared for the banquet, which followed the betrothal. It was covered with blue canvas painted with the signs of the zodiac and hung with chandeliers of candles. After the food there was a special play, called a masque, with the players dressed all in white. King Francis himself appeared in the masque, also dressed in white, with his arms outstretched. The English courtiers thought he was trying to look like Jesus.

In those days, such engagements between royal children were common. They had nothing to do with love and everything to do with power and political strategy. Throughout the reign of Henry VIII, the two big players in Europe were France and an alliance, or federation, of countries known as the Holy Roman Empire. Both powers were always seeking allies against the other among the smaller, less significant countries, of which England was one.

Four years later, the engagement between young Mary and young Francis was off. It was 1522, and that summer, at Richmond Palace, it was the turn of an important Spanish visitor to watch Princess Mary — now six years old — as she danced especially for him. She was blond and pretty, dressed like a miniature adult in silk and velvet. Mary moved gracefully, demonstrating first a slow, stately court dance and then leaping her way through an exciting fast dance with complicated steps. Her mother watched proudly, and then when Mary had finished told the child to show the visitor how well she could play the virginals, an instrument like the piano.

The visitor was the Spanish ambassador, and the reason the queen was so eager to impress him was that Henry VIII was about to make a deal with Charles V, king of Spain and Holy Roman Emperor. From now on, Henry would support Charles in his wars against Francis I, the French king. In return, 22-year-old Charles promised he would marry Mary when she grew up.

In one sense, Charles was a great catch for Mary. He was descended from four very powerful grandparents, Ferdinand II of Aragon (the father of Queen Catherine, so Mary's grandfather); Isabella of Castile; the Holy Roman Emperor Maximilian I; and Mary of Burgundy. As a result, he ruled lands that stretched the length and breadth of Europe. The Netherlands and Luxembourg formed the core of the Holy Roman Empire, to which Charles was elected emperor like his Hapsburg grandfather. But he also ruled over Aragon, Granada,

Castile, Navarre, Sicily, Sardinia, and Austria, not to mention all the Spanish conquests in South America. He had his work cut out defending and ruling all these different countries.

Henry VIII, in comparison, was just a small-fry in the power stakes, with only England to rule over, plus a small part of France to which England laid claim. However, he had been on the throne longer than his wife's nephew, and he was a much more commanding figure. Charles was very pale, with narrow eyes, a huge jaw, bad teeth, and indigestion. Henry on the other hand was tall, blond, and handsome, popular with his subjects, and a talented musician. He loved jousting and hunting, dancing, flirting, and eating.

Henry also knew how to show a guest a good time. Before Charles came to England, Henry had all the buildings on Charles's route into London painted and decorated in his honor. Pageants and tournaments were held, with the two kings riding in the lists in gorgeous livery. In the great hall at Windsor, there was a play in which a real wild horse — representing the ambition of the French king, run wild — had to be captured and tamed by the representatives of England and the Holy Roman Empire. And as always when Henry entertained, there were lavish banquets. On the day the treaty was signed and Mary became the fiancée of her grown-up cousin, England declared war on France. Having gotten what he wanted, Charles kissed her good-bye and returned to Europe.

In fact, Charles had hoped to take Mary with him to Spain, where she could be brought up as Spanish royalty. Henry refused this request. He wanted to keep his options open. If his foreign policy changed, he would need his daughter safe in England, not a hostage at the Spanish court. It was agreed that Mary would not go to Spain until she was 12. In the meantime, her mother would teach her Spanish, and her clothes would be sent from Spain, cut according to the Spanish fashion. So Mary's life did not change that much, except that she now took delivery of trunkloads of Spanish dresses, all beautifully cut to her tiny size, and grew up believing that one day, instead of being queen of France, she would be empress of the Holy Roman Empire.

Her mother, Catherine of Aragon, was delighted to think of Mary marrying back into her Spanish family. She invited a Spanish philosopher and educator named Juan Luis Vives to supervise Mary's education. Catherine herself was very well educated. She thought deeply about religion and, with Henry, discussed matters with the humanist thinkers of her day, men who studied the Greek and Roman classics and related them to Christianity. So Mary studied the Bible and Greek philosophers and learned Greek, Latin, and various modern European languages.

There was a downside to Vives's educational thinking. He believed that all women were instruments of the devil. In this he was referring back to the biblical story of Adam and Eve and viewing Eve as a temptress. In fact, many men at that time shared this belief. For them, the only point of educating their daughters at all was that it might impress upon them the importance of chastity and prepare them to be good and dutiful wives. Mary's grandmother, Isabella of Castile, had ridden at the head of an army to fight for her kingdom and given birth to Catherine in the middle of besieging Granada, but Mary was being prepared for a life in which she did what her husband told her. It was not great training for a future queen, although it probably made some sort of sense if that queen were to be married to the Holy Roman Emperor.

Mary did not see Charles again after the engagement ceremony, though she wrote to him from time to time. When she was nine, she sent him an emerald, with a message that said she hoped he was as true to her as she was to him. Charles was not remotely true to anyone, but he played along. He put the ring on his little finger and said that he would wear it for her sake. However, it was not long after this that he decided he wanted to be free to marry someone else. Gallant to the end, in word at least, he released Mary from her engagement. He sent his messengers to tell her father that he:

> . . . could have with much thank the lady princess in his hand, which is a pearl worth the keeping.

We don't know what Mary felt about the broken engagement, but very soon afterward, as if to prepare her for her role as future queen, Henry sent nine-year-old Mary to Ludlow to rule over Wales. In those days, Wales was a wild place, a very long ride from London. It was nothing new for Mary to change locations, with a train of wagons loaded with furniture, linen, gowns, and all the things needed to keep a princess happy. The royal family did it all the time, shifting from one palace or castle to another whenever the privies (toilets that were usually pits beneath a wooden seat with a hole in it) became too full and smelly. This time, however, Mary — or rather the councillors sent with her — had a job to do: namely, to bring the unruly Welsh to order, impose justice, and make them pay their taxes.

So the royal train set out westward along the rutted highways. Mary would have traveled in a litter (a carriage on poles carried by men) unless the weather was fine, when she might have ridden on horseback beside her courtiers and councillors. The roads were still too poor for coaches; only goods and luggage traveled on wooden wagons. It was several days' ride, with stops at the houses of local landowners along the way.

With Mary went her lady governess, her ladies-in-waiting, her musicians, and her tutors. For although she was to be the centerpiece of her own court, Mary's education would continue as before. In order to guarantee that she got none of the wrong ideas — even though she was only nine — all the ladies of her court were married women who dressed soberly in dark colors.

Vives disapproved of dancing, so it was discouraged and Mary spent long hours in study. For exercise she would go hunting, which she loved. In fact, one of the privileges of her position was that she could grant the right to hunt deer to whomever she wished. The rest of the time she was just a small figure surrounded by grown men who were carrying out the real business of government. Nevertheless, she learned to behave as a queen. She was representing her father, so she did as she had seen him do, offering her hand to be kissed when local dignitaries, many of whom had never seen a princess before, came and knelt before her.

For the ladies-in-waiting it was a dreary time and a far cry from Henry's colorful court, with its pageants, dancing, and love affairs. For the councillors, too, it wasn't easy. The Welsh were annoyed about paying taxes and taking orders from London, and after two years Mary was recalled to London. Once again, the wagons were loaded, the horses saddled, and the whole cumbersome procession made its way back to the capital.

Henry had been busy in Mary's absence, negotiating another marriage treaty with the French on her behalf. At first it looked as if Mary would marry the king himself this time, but Francis found himself defeated in battle by Charles V. He had to make peace, and to cement the deal he married Charles's sister, Eleanor. So Mary found herself engaged to King Francis's young son, the Duke of Orleans, once more.

Preparations for the great banquet to celebrate Mary's third betrothal went on throughout the summer of 1527. For weeks, Mary went for fittings for her new dress, shoes, and the cap that would hold her hair in place. She and seven of her ladies spent hours with the court dancing master, rehearsing the dances and the masque that were to be performed to entertain the French dignitaries. When Mary was at court, she lived according to Henry's ideas, not those of Vives.

Finally, the preparations were complete. Mary, who was now 11 years old, was very excited. Her new fiancé would not be there that evening, but the French ambassador would be watching the proceedings carefully so he could send his master a detailed description of his bride-to-be. And so he was. Like the Spanish ambassador before him, he watched Mary's every move. He noticed how assured she was as she sat at the head of her own table, surrounded by ladies and gentlemen of the French court. The banquet lasted for hours, as course after course was brought in on silver trays, to be eaten from golden plates.

It was late by the time the banquet was over and the assembled company moved into the "disguising house," a small theater specially built for the occasion. There the guests took their places strictly according to importance and rank, with the ladies on one side of the room and the gentlemen on the other. The room was brightly lit, with great chandeliers of candles. There were songs from the children of the king's chapel and a mock tournament, and then it was time for Princess Mary to take her place on the silk-carpeted stage. She and seven other girls wore dresses of gold cloth, their hair wound with jewels. They performed an intricate dance against a backdrop of mountains studded with gems. Eight young men in golden doublets (jackets) held flaming torches to light the scene.

Like her father, Mary was energetic and light on her feet. One observer said that with all her jewels and the excitement of the occasion, she "dazzled the sight" that evening. After the dancing was over, the girls crowded around Mary's father, who was a tall, handsome man of 36, still slim and attractive. Henry pulled his daughter aside and beckoned the French ambassador to him. He pulled off the netted jeweled cap that held Mary's hair in place and let her long hair, golden-red like his own, tumble down her back. It was clear that he was proud of her. He loved her, and he wanted the French to see what a jewel they were getting. Mary basked in his admiration.

Poor Mary. What she did not know, in those years when she seemed to be the apple of her father's eye, was that he was a disappointed man. Queen Catherine had been pregnant many times, but always the child died, either in the womb or shortly after it was born. Henry was grateful to have a living daughter, but no daughter would ever be good enough. He was king of England, and he needed a son to succeed him.

He wasn't alone in thinking this. In those days, kings still led their armies into battle, which most women were unable to do, although there were exceptions like Mary's grandmother, Isabella of Castile. Many men believed that women were incapable of ruling a kingdom, and the last time a woman had inherited the English throne (Matilda, in 1135), civil war had broken out immediately.

Also in English law, all women were the subjects of their husbands. If they owned property, it became their husband's on marriage. They had to do what their husbands told them, and if they didn't their husbands were free to beat them or punish them any way they saw fit. This didn't sit very well with trying to rule a kingdom.

Henry brooded on these things. By the time Mary was six, he had already taken advice on what the legal position would be if his daughter were to inherit the throne. A couple of serious accidents when he was in his thirties brought his worries into sharper focus. In a jousting tournament, a lance splintered and he nearly lost an eye. Not long afterward, Henry fell facedown in a ditch while hunting and had to be hauled out by his courtiers. What would have happened if they hadn't saved him? Especially as, with every year that passed, it seemed less and less likely that Catherine, who was five years older than Henry, would bear him a son.

In fact, Henry already had a son, a boy three years younger than Mary. His mother had been a lady-in-waiting of Queen Catherine's named Bessie Blount. Catherine had been very upset when Bessie became pregnant and sent her away from court. It was galling for her when Bessie's child turned out to be a healthy boy. Henry was pleased. The child was christened Henry and given the surname traditional for the illegitimate children of kings — Fitzroy. (Fitz means "son of" and roy is from the French word *roi*, for "king.") Henry found an obliging nobleman named Gilbert Tallboys who was willing to marry Bessie. However, everyone at court referred to Bessie as "the mother of the king's son," which naturally annoyed Catherine.

And Henry treated the boy as his son. At the same time that he sent Mary to rule over Wales, he made her half brother Earl of Nottingham and Duke of Richmond and Somerset. And when Mary was promised to the Duke of Orleans, Henry Fitzroy was promised to the Duke's sister. Queen Catherine didn't like this. She herself was a royal princess, the daughter of King Ferdinand of Aragon. She didn't like the illegitimate son of some upstart courtier being treated on a par with her daughter. When she complained to her husband, he sent her away from court to teach her a lesson.

In those days, the rules were quite clear. Everyone knew that the king could have children with whomever he liked, but the only children who counted, when it came to succession to the throne, were those born to the queen. But Henry was getting desperate. He knew that Catherine would not bear him a son. And he knew that to leave his kingdom to Mary would mean effectively that her husband — probably a foreign prince — would become England's king. To Henry, who was proud to be English and to have ruled England well, this seemed a terrible fate. He didn't want to leave his country to be just one of a dozen countries ruled by some foreign prince. And the more powerful the man Mary married, the more likely that would happen.

On the other hand, to bypass Mary and make his illegitimate son his heir would cause trouble, not least because Catherine, as a Spanish princess, had powerful allies. What Henry needed was a *legitimate* male heir.

The issue continued to worry Henry year after year. He began to believe that God was punishing him. All Catherine's dead babies were a curse, he thought; a punishment for something he and Catherine had done wrong. And the more Henry thought about it, the more he became convinced that the thing they had done wrong was to marry in the first place.

Catherine had come to England as a young girl of 15 to marry Henry's older brother, Arthur, who was then 13. The two had married but had lived separately. Arthur was a puny child, very small for his age, and the parents were waiting for him to grow up before he and Catherine lived as man and wife. Then, very suddenly, he died, probably of what was known as the sweating sickness, a mysterious illness that killed most people who caught it within days. After his death, Catherine remained in England, a widow who had never actually been a wife, while arguments raged between her father-in-law, Henry VII, and her own father, Ferdinand. There was talk of her marrying Arthur's younger brother, Henry, who was tall, healthy, and handsome. But Ferdinand refused to give a second dowry (he thought the first one should count), and Henry VII said that the marriage was out of the question unless he did. Over time, Catherine became so poor that she had almost nothing to eat and nothing to wear. Meanwhile, Henry VII, who was an extremely strict father, refused his son permission to see her.

Then Henry VII died, and within weeks, Catherine's fortunes changed. Henry VIII, who was just 18 to Catherine's 23, offered to marry her. He was probably in love with her, for she was small, pretty, and very plucky, and, like him, she had had a raw deal from his harsh father.

However, it was against Church law for a man to marry his brother's widow, so Henry had to get permission from the pope. Permission was granted on the grounds that the first couple had never been together. Catherine and all her ladies of the bedchamber, including a very fierce Spanish matron called Doña Elvira, had sworn at the time that this was the case. Now, twenty years later, Henry decided it was probably a lie. He believed that the death of Catherine's babies proved that he, and England, were being punished for a sinful marriage. The only solution, thought Henry, was to go back to the pope, tell him what had happened, and ask him to annul his marriage to Catherine (officially declaring that they had never truly been married in the sight of God).

This was not the first time a case like this had arisen. Normally, the pope was fairly obliging about allowing *and* annulling royal marriages. The pope understood the need for a son as well as anyone. In fact, there had been talk of him allowing Princess Mary to marry her half brother, Henry Fitzroy, in order to provide England with a stable monarchy, which really would have been bending the rules. However, in this case there was a problem. Rome had been overrun by the Holy Roman Emperor's forces, and the current pope was a prisoner of Charles V. And Charles V was the nephew of Queen Catherine. There was no way the pope could do as Henry asked, without bringing the wrath of the emperor down upon himself.

Henry had probably reached his conclusions about his marriage on his own, through reading the Bible and talking to churchmen. But by the time the Pope — and Catherine — heard about it, Henry had met the woman who was to change his life and alter the course of English history.

The King's Great Matter

ANNE BOLEYN WAS a young Englishwoman who had spent some time at the French court, acting as lady-in-waiting to Queen Claude of France. The French court was the most sophisticated court in Europe at the time. Great painters and sculptors such as Leonardo da Vinci and Benvenuto Cellini worked there, and the king's sister acted as patron to famous writers. So when Anne came back to England she brought a bit of French sophistication with her.

Anne was young, pretty, and headstrong, with long black hair and huge dark eyes, and Henry was bewitched. In fact, many of her enemies, who couldn't see why she was different from all the other girls he'd fallen for, believed she actually *was* a witch. This was unfair. Anne clearly was special. She was clever and cultured. It was a time when many reformists were questioning the way the Church behaved and suggesting ways in which it might be reformed. Anne was genuinely interested in their ideas, long before Henry started to side with them for his own private reasons. She sent to Europe for new translations of the Bible. She loved discussion and debate. But, unlike many of the reformists — who were later known as Protestants — she also loved music, dancing, and rich clothes.

Henry loved her for her intelligence and passion and spirit. Anne soon realized the hold she had over the king and was determined to use it to her advantage. She was not going to be tossed aside with nothing to show for it, the way her sister had been when the king dropped her after a brief affair. So she told Henry she loved him but stopped short of being with him. Then she took herself off to her father's house in Kent, leaving Henry desperate to do whatever it took to make her change her mind. She told him there was only one thing that would make her do that, and that was marriage. For Henry, the prospect of marriage to Anne was very attractive, not least because she was young and might give him a son. The only obstacle in his way — and it was a big one — was the fact that he was still married to Catherine.

Henry excelled at most things in life — sports, music, dancing, government, and winning women. The one thing he didn't much like doing was writing. But he was madly in love, and when Anne disappeared from court, Henry wrote her letter after letter, struggling, in clumsy handwriting, to be the courtly lover he thought she wanted. (The letters are still in the Vatican Library in Rome, which probably shows how seriously the Church viewed the affair.) And he sent his councillors to Rome to put his case for divorce to the pope.

It wasn't that Henry disliked Catherine. They had been married a long time, and he was still fond of her. A lot of people think he was a little in awe of her because she was virtuous in a way that he, with his hot temper and all his infidelities, could never be. But they had failed to produce a male heir, the one thing that a royal couple must do, and therefore he thought they should agree to go their separate ways, saying and doing whatever was needed to achieve this. And he expected her to agree with him.

Catherine, however, was having nothing to do with Henry's plan. She was a deeply religious, loyal wife, and she found the idea insulting. Also, she knew what the consequences would be for Mary. If her marriage to Henry was annulled, any children of that marriage would become illegitimate. Catherine refused to let that happen. So for a number of years, the argument rumbled on. People spoke of it as "the king's Great Matter." Catherine was still queen and accompanied Henry on state occasions. Behind the scenes, Henry spent all his time with Anne. Sometimes he would have dinner with Catherine to try to persuade her of the justness of his cause. He had, he said, many religious experts who would speak in favor of his case. Catherine retorted that she could produce ten experts for every one of his.

Perhaps Catherine thought that the problem would

blow over; that Henry's passion for Anne would cool and that they would go on as before. The pope was certainly hoping so. He did not want to turn down Henry point-blank. Henry had been a good Christian king (in 1521 the pope had given him the title Defender of the Faith). So he delayed the decision in the hope that Henry would forget about marrying Anne. Meanwhile, Henry hoped that the pope would escape from the clutches of Charles V.

Neither happened. It was a stalemate. Many people, including his chancellor, Sir Thomas More, and John Fisher, Bishop of Rochester, thought Henry was in the wrong. But as time went on it became clear to everyone — except for Catherine's closest allies — that the wisest course for the queen would be to agree to what Henry asked and retire to a convent. Catherine refused. She had a stubborn streak — which her daughter inherited — and went on repeating her arguments over and over again to anyone who would listen until many people were sick of them.

It was now 1532, six years since Anne had first caught the king's eye, and she was becoming impatient. Finally, Henry decided to take matters into his own hands. He set up a commission to look into the right of the pope to decide Church law in England. Henry himself led the commission, so it wasn't surprising that the commissioners found that the pope had no business interfering with English law. From now on, it was decided, Henry himself would be Supreme Head on Earth of the Church of

England. This, naturally, meant that all previous decisions, such as the one that said it was all right for Henry to marry his brother's widow, were suspect. More important still, Henry himself could now reverse the decision.

What this did was effectively make a lifelong enemy of Charles V, which automatically meant that France became Henry's natural ally. In October 1532, Henry made a public statement by taking Anne as his consort (effectively queen) to meet the French king at Boulogne. Francis I also had a new consort, following the death of Queen Claude. The new French queen was Eleanor, sister of Charles V and a niece of Catherine of Aragon. She refused to meet Anne, but the French king realized that recognition of Anne was the price of Henry's support. He gave a banquet in their honor. Anne was now sure that Henry had come too far to turn back. By the end of the year she gave him some very good news: She was pregnant. Henry was delighted. If she produced a boy, it would show the world that he had been right in putting Catherine aside.

Anne's pregnancy also meant that there could be no more delay about the divorce. Henry made sure that the new Archbishop of Canterbury, Thomas Cranmer, knew he held his position only with Henry's agreement. And Anne Boleyn appeared in public at court and dropped a big hint by saying that "she had a furious hankering to eat apples, such as she had never had in her life before." Then she laughed and left, leaving the courtiers to draw their own conclusions.

In fact, Henry and Anne had already married, secretly. And in May 1533, Archbishop Cranmer announced that the marriage between Henry and Catherine had never been legal, so the marriage between Henry and Anne was sound. On the last day of May, Anne Boleyn went to her coronation six months pregnant.

Anne Boleyn had many good qualities, but sensitivity to Catherine's feelings was not among them. She commandeered the ex-queen's barge for the occasion, with her own coat of arms nailed where Catherine's had been just the previous week. Her dress had been let out specially for the occasion, and her long dark hair, so long she could sit on it, hung loose.

Henry spent a fortune on the coronation. He had persuaded himself that he was acting in the best interests of England. He wanted everyone to share his triumph and his hope that the child Anne was carrying would be a son. So a flotilla of small ships and barges, flying brightly colored taffeta flags and decked with gold, escorted the new queen to the Tower of London on the eve of her coronation. As the little fleet arrived at the Tower, there were gun salutes so loud they broke the glass in nearby windows.

On the day of the coronation, Anne rode in a litter completely covered in white satin and drawn by a pair of white horses. She wore a white dress and a white cloak trimmed with the white fur of ermine. Before her rode knights and merchants, all dressed in silk, velvet, and taffeta. Behind her rode the ladies of the court, dressed in gowns of gold and red. Along the route of the procession, tapestries and carpets hung from the windows that overlooked the narrow streets. The trade guilds (associations of skilled workmen such as stonemasons, carpenters, tailors, and cobblers) dutifully put on pageants. Choirs of children sang, and poems were read in her honor. But all the money in the world couldn't conceal the fact that most people thought the wedding was a scandal. Several noblemen had found pressing reasons why they couldn't be in London that day. The crowds were thin, there was little cheering, and many men kept on their hats as the new queen passed. There were jokes about the queen's big belly, and a lot of people noted what the beautifully intertwining initials *H* and *A* spelled. They nudged each other cynically and said, "Ha-ha!" There was even an occasional daring cry of "God save Queen Catherine."

The truth was that Anne Boleyn was deeply unpopular. She was seen as a gold digger, an ambitious upstart who didn't even know how to behave like royalty. When the guildsmen presented her with purses of gold coins, Anne didn't distribute them to her guard, as "real" royalty would have done. She kept them for herself. Even the beautiful dark eyes that had so captivated Henry were mocked by the onlookers at the wedding.

Anne had none of the powerful international connections that Catherine had. All she had going for her was the fact she was young, intelligent, pretty, and — most important of all — able to have children. All her hopes — and Henry's — depended on the baby in her belly. Anne was so sure of her luck that she drew up an announcement ahead of time, declaring the birth of a prince.

In September 1533, the baby was born. It was a girl. She was christened Elizabeth. Henry was so disappointed that he didn't even bother to attend her christening and canceled the tournament planned to celebrate the birth. There were none of the customary bonfires in the streets. But whatever the king and the people of England felt, there had come into the world a baby girl whose very existence would put Mary's position in jeopardy for the rest of her life.

Pushed Aside

THROUGHOUT HER TEENAGE YEARS, Mary had watched as the father she loved insulted and hurt her beloved mother. For Mary, as for the rest of her mother's family, it was outrageous that Henry should think of putting aside Catherine. Catherine had been a good and faithful wife who had wanted nothing more than a whole nursery full of royal princes and princesses. She had suffered terribly with the deaths of her babies. She was also a princess from one of the most powerful royal houses in Europe. It was just wrong in Mary's eyes that her mother should be cast aside for a "commoner" — someone who had no royal blood.

And it was also an insult to her religion. Perhaps Mary would have disliked reformists even if Anne Boleyn had never existed, but the way that Henry used religion to justify his own willful purpose added a whole new dimension to her dislike.

Above all, Mary hated Anne. She called her "that concubine" and blamed her for leading her father astray. As far as Mary was concerned, it was Anne's fault that her father was divorcing her mother. It was Anne's fault that her father was putting his immortal soul in danger by going against the true Catholic Church. It was Anne's fault that her father now refused to see her, and Anne's fault that he forbade her to see her mother. Mary may even have been right in thinking this. She was firmly on her mother's side, and a reproachful daughter was all too likely to make Henry feel guilty. Anne didn't want that, and neither did Henry.

In the spring of 1533, Mary received a letter from her father. In it he told her that he had married Anne Boleyn and that from now on Mary was not even allowed to write to her mother. Mary was horrified. She knew how much her mother depended on her, and she wanted a chance to write at least one last letter to Catherine, explaining why she could no longer contact her. Henry refused.

Then the baby arrived. All her life, Mary had tried to behave like a good Christian, but it's difficult to imagine that in these circumstances she felt anything but deep satisfaction when she heard that the baby was a girl. It was certainly a kick in the teeth for Anne, who had caused her mother such grief. And a girl should have posed no threat to Mary's claim to the throne of England. According to the law of succession, boys always preceded girls, but where there were only girls, they succeeded in age order, eldest first.

Henry, however, was about to break the rules again. The new baby would supplant Mary in every way. She was given the title of Princess Royal, which had been Mary's title. She was very nearly given the name Mary, something that usually only happened when an older sister of the same name had died. It was as close to being rubbed out of the family as was possible without actually being killed. (In fact, the Spanish ambassador, Eustace Chapuys, was convinced that this was what Henry meant to do to Mary.)

Within days of Elizabeth's birth, Mary was informed by the Duke of Norfolk that she was now only "Lady Mary." He spoke of baby Elizabeth as "the Princess Royal." Mary was furious. "That is a title that belongs to me by right, and to no one else," she said. She went on to say that, as Henry acknowledged Elizabeth as his child, she would address Elizabeth as sister, but she would never call her princess. She wrote letters to Henry, signing herself "princess" and, even more boldly, sent verbal messages to him from "The Princess Royal."

Mary's defiance enraged Anne and made Henry determined to bring her to heel. She was moved, at half an hour's notice, to Elizabeth's house at Hatfield. Her own household of loyal Catholic servants was disbanded. Not even her godmother, Margaret Pole, who had looked after her from birth, was allowed to go with her. The horses that she loved to ride were left behind. Her jewels were taken from her and given to Elizabeth. The Spanish ambassador described the room she was given at Hatfield as "the worst lodging in the house." She was even expected to curtsy to her baby half sister.

The next eight months saw a battle of wills between Mary and the courtiers of Elizabeth's household. Mary refused to come out of her room to eat because it meant sitting beneath Elizabeth at the table. She refused to call her princess. When they went out, Elizabeth was carried in a velvet litter, while Mary had to walk beside her. One time, when the whole household was moving to a new house, she refused to ride behind Elizabeth in procession. Mary was forcibly dragged from her room and bundled into a litter. Anne was furious about this behavior and gave instructions that every time Mary acted up, she was to be given a good box on the ears. After that, Mary was punished each time, often by having her clothes taken from her, until she was down to almost nothing.

Elizabeth's household consisted almost entirely of Boleyn supporters, but there were people among them who felt sorry for Mary. One young maid carried messages between Mary and the Spanish ambassador, mostly letters for her mother. The maid was caught and threatened with imprisonment in the Tower of London. She confessed and was fired.

Queen Anne often visited Elizabeth, and on one visit she summoned Mary to see her. She told Mary that she would be welcome at court provided she acknowledged Anne as queen. "I know no Queen but my mother," Mary told Anne coldly. Anne left in a fury, cursing Mary's proud Spanish blood. Anne swore she would make Mary give in if it was the last thing she did.

It was the only time that Mary and Anne came face-to-face. Usually Mary was locked in her room when Henry and Anne came to visit Elizabeth. Mary found this unbearable. Once when Henry was in the house, Mary sent a message to him, begging him to let her come and kiss his hand. Henry ignored her request, but as he and Anne, ready to leave, mounted their horses, he happened to glance up at a balcony. There was Mary, kneeling, her arms outstretched, silently begging him to acknowledge her. Henry nodded gruffly and touched his hat. Then he rode on his way.

What Henry wanted from Mary was the same thing he had wanted from her mother. He wanted her to fall in quietly with his version of events. He wanted Mary to say his marriage to her mother had been illegal, that she herself was illegitimate, and that Anne was his legal wife, and Anne's child — or, as Henry still hoped, children — were the legitimate heirs to Henry's throne.

But Mary refused to do what Henry wanted. Partly this was because of loyalty to her mother. Mary also felt it was wrong of her father to rewrite history just to suit himself. *And* she was a loyal Catholic. Mary had been brought up to believe that the pope was God's representative on Earth and that no one, not even a king, was above him. The various acts that Henry had brought into being and put before Parliament after he married Anne Boleyn left the pope out of the picture. To fall in behind Henry would to be disloyal to the pope and to the religion in which she believed wholeheartedly. There was no way Mary was going to do it.

There were many people in England who felt like Mary. They, too, were suffering for what Henry saw as their stubbornness. As soon as he had married Anne, Henry had introduced a number of acts to Parliament, changing the law so that what he had done was legal. The first of these was the Act of Appeals, which put Henry at the head of the Church.

"This realm of England is an Empire, governed by one Head and King," it began, and went on to say that the king had the authority to decide on matters, including religious issues, "without the intermeddling of any exterior person." This was a direct attack on the pope's authority. A second act made Henry the judge of when it was all right to depart from Church law. Another said that the dues that the bishops used to pay to the pope would in future be paid to the crown; and another act said that the priests and bishops were subject to the ordinary laws of England. Finally, the Act of Succession made Mary officially illegitimate and named Elizabeth as Henry's heir.

Worse still for Mary, all the most important and prominent people in the country were asked to swear on oath that they accepted the Act of Succession. Many of them refused to sign this oath, among them John Fisher,

Bishop of Rochester, and Sir Thomas More, former Chancellor of the Realm. They were put in prison, awaiting trial for treason. Mary was told that if she didn't sign, the same thing would happen to her.

In 1535, a few days after she was told about these arrests, Mary fell seriously ill. Perhaps it was due to stress, coming after two years of bullying and petty cruelty. Henry was told how ill she was. He did absolutely nothing for six days. He may have been hoping Mary would die and relieve him of the problem of what to do with her. Finally, worried about what Charles V might think, he summoned the Spanish ambassador, Eustace Chapuys, and invited him to bring Spanish doctors to see Mary.

In fact, no doctor, Spanish or English, wanted to be involved in Mary's treatment. They knew that however much Henry secretly hoped she would die, he was liable to turn on whoever had treated her if she did. Besides, they all agreed, it might well be that the conditions in which she was held and anxiety about her future were at the root of the problem. She lived in fear of her life, isolated among enemies, and she was not allowed to see or write to her mother or even the Spanish ambassador. Other people whispered that it was not just neglect and fear that were wrong with Mary; they believed she had been poisoned — Queen Anne had often threatened to get rid of Mary once and for all.

Queen Catherine was desperately worried about Mary. She wrote to Henry, begging him to allow her to nurse her daughter. Henry refused. So Mary lay close to death in a house where the doctors were afraid to treat her and where people said openly, in her hearing, that it would be a good thing if she died. The king had said much the same thing to the Spanish ambassador. It was true that the Holy Roman Emperor would make a fuss, but Henry believed it would blow over, and with Mary gone, there would be no rival to Elizabeth's claim to the throne.

The fact was that Henry was afraid of the amount of support in the country for his ex-wife and his daughter. He knew that whenever Mary went anywhere, small groups of people gathered to watch her pass. This was why he did not want her in touch with her mother. He was secretly afraid of Catherine. For one thing, Catherine had a claim to the throne of England in her own right, as she was descended from Edward III (1327 – 1377) through one of his younger sons, John of Gaunt. For another, she was the daughter of Isabella of Castile, who had ridden at the head of an army. In Henry's mind, it always remained a possibility that Catherine might follow her mother's example and raise a rebellion against him.

In fact, Catherine was too loyal ever to do such a thing. Instead she remained under house arrest, imprisoned in her house at Kimbolton, worrying herself sick about Mary and wishing she could help. Mary, against all the odds and in the face of angry letters from her father telling her she was his worst enemy, began to get well.

Meanwhile, the situation in the country was becoming worse for Catholics. In the spring of 1535, three monks who had refused to sign the Oath of Succession were convicted of treason and hanged at Tyburn. In the weeks that followed, more monks were tortured and hanged. Then John Fisher, Bishop of Rochester and now a cardinal, was beheaded. (Fisher had written to Charles V begging him to invade the country and depose Henry, to save the Catholic Church in England and the lives of Catherine and Mary.) Thomas More, Henry's former chancellor, followed Fisher to the block. These executions and the torture of other men in Henry's prisons caused outrage all over Europe. Even Protestants in Germany condemned Henry's tyranny. Then, the same year, it rained all summer, ruining the harvest. Most of the people were still Catholics at heart and began to talk of the curse Henry had brought on the country.

Fisher had not been alone in hoping that Charles V would invade England. Catherine herself wrote to the pope, saying, "We await a remedy from God and Your Holiness." There were plans afoot on the part of the Spanish to rescue her and Mary. But these came too late for Catherine. Years of rejection and misery had aged her. She lived, a prisoner in a drafty, neglected manor house, seeing almost no one and cut off from the daughter she loved.

As Mary's long recovery continued, she learned that her mother had gone into decline. Catherine had been known all her life for her charity. Now she had nothing to give to her servants. She wrote to the king, begging him to give them a year's wages, since she could not. In her last message to Henry, she told him that she forgave him everything and asked him to look after Mary. She spent her last hours in prayer.

No sympathy was shown to Mary, either by her father or by Elizabeth's servants. Lady Shelton, Elizabeth's governess and great-aunt, told her brusquely that her mother had died. Mary wanted to speak to Catherine's doctor, to find out whether he suspected poison. It must have been hard for Mary to hear that he did; and hard, too, to know that her father had thrown a party to celebrate her mother's death. The Spanish ambassador described Henry dressed from head to foot in yellow, with a white feather in his hat, as he went to church to give thanks, carrying Elizabeth in his arms. Afterward he danced and jousted like a man half his age.

With Catherine no longer there to argue, Henry was able to have things all his own way at her funeral. Mary, who might also have had something to say, was still in disgrace, so the mourners were led by Henry's niece Eleanor as the coffin was taken to the Benedictine Abbey at Peterborough. There Catherine lay in state, in a lead-lined coffin packed with spices to make the body smell sweet, and lit by a thousand candles. Around her hung the flags of the many royal houses of Europe from which she was descended. But despite the apparent honor, Henry was making a point. The only sign of her connection to the royal house of England was the coat of arms of the long-dead Arthur; and instead of a queen's crown there was only a princess's coronet. To ram the point home, the bishop who delivered the funeral address told the mourners that on her deathbed Catherine had finally admitted that Henry had been right all along. She had never been legally married to him or entitled to call herself queen. The mourners were not fooled. Many of them prayed out loud for Queen Catherine.

Unlike Henry, the Holy Roman Emperor put on black when he heard of Catherine's death. He was genuinely sorry his aunt was gone and shocked by Henry's cruelty toward her, but secretly he, too, was relieved. He had not wanted to go to war over Catherine. He was certainly not going to war over Mary, whom he regarded as a very minor player. So Mary's position looked bleaker than ever. Now grieving for her mother and without allies, it seemed it would only be a matter of time before her own father had her murdered.

No wonder Mary hated Anne Boleyn and her child, Elizabeth, who had brought such terror and grief into her life.

Elizabeth
Princess No More
1535 – 1537

ELIZABETH WAS STILL only a baby, of course. None of what had happened to Mary was her fault, and she was too young to have on opinion of it. It was not her doing that Mary, like everyone who came into her presence apart from her father and mother, had to curtsy to her. As she grew from infancy to being a toddler, she must have become aware of the shouting and the scenes. She would have picked up on the dislike her half sister felt toward her. To Elizabeth, Mary must have seemed like the bad fairy at the christening party.

In those days, royal children lived apart from their parents, each in their own household (which is why it had been such an issue for Mary when hers was disbanded). Henry and Anne often visited Elizabeth, cuddling her and making a fuss of her. Anne made sure that she was dressed in fine clothes, made by her French tailor, often in shades of green or yellow, which suited her red hair. Like Mary before her, Elizabeth was officially heir to the throne and the apple of her father's eye.

However, there were people at court who knew how precarious Elizabeth's position really was. Henry had fallen out of love with Anne Boleyn, and the couple was getting on very badly. On the very day Queen Catherine was buried, Anne had suffered a miscarriage. The baby, had it lived, would have been a boy. Henry was furious, and Anne was terrified. She knew that Henry was already looking at other women. Anne was a fiery woman; she objected to this, whereupon Henry told her she would have to put up with it as "her betters" — by which he meant Catherine of Aragon — had done before her. Now she had failed again to do the one thing that would have made her position secure. She had not produced a son.

Once more, Henry saw Anne's miscarriage as God's judgment on him. He wanted to get rid of her, and he already knew who he wanted to marry next, a shy girl named Jane Seymour, who was maid of honor to the queen. Jane had her own opinions about what had been going on at court and felt very sorry for Mary. She was much too straightforward to play the sort of games Anne had played, and was now playing again. Foolishly, Anne thought she might win Henry back by making him jealous.

It was a terrible miscalculation. It had worked when Henry was madly in love and pursuing her. As his wife, however, she would be accused of treason, and the penalty for treason was death. With Catherine newly in her grave, this suited Henry. He didn't want another ex-wife, arguing about her rights and the rights of her daughter. This was his chance to start afresh as a widower.

On May 2, 1536, Anne was arrested and accused of adultery with half a dozen courtiers, including the musician Mark Smeaton and her own brother, the Earl of Rochford. It was a put-up job, and there was never any doubt that they would all be found guilty. In the two weeks before her execution, Henry went partying every night and could be heard singing with his companions as the royal barge sailed home to Greenwich Palace.

Anne's alleged boyfriends were tortured to make them confess. Naturally, they said what Henry wanted them to say, and Anne's fate was sealed. She was terrified that Henry would exact the usual penalty for an adulterous queen and have her burned at the stake. Instead, she begged for a French-style execution, where the executioner used a sword instead of an ax. Henry granted her wish. A French executioner was sent for, and Anne was executed on May 19, 1536. Among the spectators was Henry Fitzroy, the king's illegitimate son. (Anne had not liked him because he posed a threat to Elizabeth's claim to the throne.) Now that Anne was dead, he must have thought he had a good chance of becoming the heir. In fact, he, too, would be dead within the year.

The day of Anne's death, Henry dressed himself all in white, so that no one would think he was mourning, and went to see Jane Seymour. Preparations for a third wedding were begun. A new Act of Succession was drawn up.

As well as executing Anne, Henry's priests proclaimed that his marriage to her had never been legal. This made nonsense of the charge that she had committed adultery, but it ensured that Jane's children were the only ones with a valid claim to the throne. For now Elizabeth was in the same position as Mary, and indeed Henry Fitzroy. They were all illegitimate. Like Mary before her, Elizabeth plummeted overnight from being Princess Royal and heir to the throne of England to being mere Lady Elizabeth.

Elizabeth was only two years and eight months old at the time, but she had been surrounded by arguments about titles, curtsying, and who went first from the time she was born. She knew these things mattered. The first time she was addressed differently she is reported to have said to the governor of her household, "How haps it, Governor, yesterday my Lady Princess and today but my Lady Elizabeth?" The governor had no answer to give her.

There were other changes, too. First of all, there were no more visits from the slim woman with the long black hair and big dark eyes who cuddled her and brought her clothes and toys, nor from her father. Henry couldn't bear to see Elizabeth after he had disposed of her mother. Her household was reduced to 32 servants. Furthermore, Mary was not allowed to live there.

The supply of beautiful clothes made by Anne's French tailor in bright, rich fabrics dried up. Elizabeth's nurse,

Lady Bryan, had to write to Henry, telling him that Elizabeth had outgrown all her clothes and that she had "neither gown, nor kirtle [skirt], nor petticoat nor no manner of linen nor smocks nor kerchiefs." There were fights about whether she should eat with everyone else or be allowed to eat privately as she had done as a princess.

Did Elizabeth remember these things when she was grown up? Many historians think she did not. Elizabeth never spoke about her mother or her death. But we know that four years after Anne's death, Elizabeth was devastated when Henry executed another wife. Also, some historians have linked Elizabeth's vast wardrobe when she was queen — she had three thousand dresses and two hundred capes — to the humiliation she felt as a three-year-old no-longer-princess with nothing to wear.

Anne had been dead less than a month when Henry married Jane Seymour. This marriage made for a happier time all around. Jane felt sorry for little motherless Elizabeth. In time she encouraged Henry to see her and made sure her servants had enough money to run the household.

A year later, Jane was expecting a baby, and in October 1537 she gave birth to a boy. Henry was triumphant. The boy was healthy, legitimate, and brought to an end all the arguments surrounding the succession. Elizabeth was at Hampton Court when he was born, together with her big sister, Mary. A few days later, they both attended the christening. Elizabeth was put in charge of the christening robe, which was too heavy for her to carry. She was carried by Jane's brother, the Earl of Hertford, who took the weight of the robe. After the ceremony, Elizabeth walked out of the chapel holding Mary's hand. The rivalry between them appeared to be over. The sisters were now good friends.

Unfortunately, even as Elizabeth's baby brother was being christened, Jane was dying. Childbirth was always dangerous in those days, and Jane had needed an operation to deliver her baby. The chances of surviving such an operation were slim. There were no anesthetics and no proper hygiene. The queen developed a raging infection. Twelve days after Edward was born, his mother was dead. Henry was heartbroken. He swore she was the only woman he had ever truly loved, but maybe that was because he hadn't had time to grow tired of her. She was buried in the royal chapel at Windsor. Beside her lay an empty stone, awaiting Henry when it was his time to die.

Nevertheless, Henry had his male heir. Mary and Elizabeth were sent back to their respective royal palaces, while Lady Bryan stayed behind to take care of the all-important baby prince. Elizabeth was given a new governess, Kat Champernowne, who later married and became known as Kat Ashley. Kat was a mother to Elizabeth for the remainder of her childhood. Stepmothers would come and go, but Kat was always there, devoted and kind, though not always very wise, throughout Elizabeth's life.

Bullied into Submission

1536 – 1537

MARY'S PROBLEMS WERE far from over when Jane Seymour replaced the beheaded Anne Boleyn as queen. Henry would not forgive Mary easily for siding with her mother. Every tantrum she had had over her royal title, every refusal to recognize that Anne was queen rankled with him. Queen Jane might feel sorry for Mary, but Henry did not. During the 23 years he had been on the English throne, Henry had become an absolute tyrant. His own daughter had dared to contradict him. As far as he was concerned, if Mary was to come back to court, she was going to have to crawl.

Henry's chief minister at this time was Thomas Cromwell. He advised Mary to write to her father, begging forgiveness. In fact, he probably wrote the letter, which began: "In as humble and lowly manner as it is possible for a child to use to her father and sovereign lord," and then went on to say that Mary knew how much she had offended Henry, acknowledged she was to blame, and begged her father to forgive her. When this drew no response, she followed it with a second, even more groveling, letter.

It still wasn't enough for Henry. He gave instructions to the Duke of Norfolk and several other commissioners in a document that talked about Henry's own gracious and divine nature. He spoke of Mary's defiant behavior as something completely unnatural, which could only be put down to the "imbecility of her sex." This stupidity, said Henry, was the only thing that enabled him even to think about forgiving her. Norfolk and the others were sent to tell Mary that the only way forward was for her to spell out the ways in which she had been wrong: She was to say her mother's marriage had been illegal, that she was illegitimate, and that the pope was not and should never have been head of the Church in England.

Mary was not prepared to do this. She repeated what she had said all along, that she would obey her father in everything but things that affected her mother's honor, her own, or her faith. The commissioners were afraid to return to Henry with this message. They shouted at Mary, trying to frighten her into changing her mind. Norfolk told her that if she were his own daughter he would beat her to death, and he threatened to throw her against a wall until her head was "as soft as a boiled apple." Coming from Norfolk, this was no idle threat. He had had his own wife tied up and beaten for objecting to the fact that he had a mistress.

Mary must have been terrified of these loud, violent men, but she refused to budge, and the commissioners had no choice but to return to Henry with the bad news. Henry flew into a rage and took his anger out on everyone, sending Mary's friend, Lady Hussey, to the Tower and threatening to have Cromwell executed. Then he decided enough was enough. He was going to put Mary on trial for treason.

Fortunately for Mary, the royal justices were not happy with this. They proposed that Mary be given time to reconsider her position and drew up a document called Lady Mary's Submission, which was sent to Hunsdon Manor for Mary to sign. In it she had to agree to the three things Henry wanted, and for good measure she had to beg for Henry's forgiveness all over again.

It was Mary's last chance to save her life. Everyone could see it. In fact, almost everyone thought she was plain pigheaded not to have agreed to what Henry wanted so far. Only Chapuys, the Spanish ambassador, could see what a terrible dilemma she was in, forced to betray her mother and her Church to save her life. To help her, he made sure that the pope understood what was going on. He told her not to read the document before she signed, so her conscience would be clear. And he also pointed out another very good reason why she should sign. Jane had not yet had her baby. Mary was still — possibly — heir to the throne. If she died, she could never become queen of England. If she lived, she might. And as queen she would be able to restore the Catholic faith and the power of the pope.

This argument worked as nothing else had done. Mary signed the submission. She was doing it not for herself but for her faith and her country. And one day it would all bear fruit.

The following summer, Mary was invited to court to meet her father again. They had not seen each other for five years. Mary saw a man heavier and older than the father she remembered. And Henry saw a self-possessed woman of 20. She was small like her mother, and she had her mother's surprisingly deep voice. She was thin and tired from illness and worry, and people at this time also commented on her peering eyes. In an age when spectacles had not yet been invented, Mary was extremely shortsighted.

Very nervous, she curtsied before Henry in front of all his courtiers. Henry took her hand and raised her up. "Some of you were desirous that I should put this jewel to death," he said to the court.

"That had been great pity to have lost your chiefest jewel of England," said Jane Seymour, now his queen.

At which, Mary is reported to have fainted.

From that moment on, it looked as if Mary was restored to favor. Henry decreed she could have a large household of her own, separate from Elizabeth's.

Immediately, his ministers were inundated with requests from people who had served her or her mother in the past, wanting to serve her again. He gave her a thousand gold coins, and Mary began to dress in the bright colors and beautiful fabrics she adored. She was allowed to appear at court and was often seen on public occasions with Henry and Jane, and for the first time since she was a child, Henry claimed to be looking for a husband for her.

And yet, all was not as it seemed. Perhaps Henry had heard what Chapuys had told the pope about Mary's real beliefs. Perhaps it was the fact that she seemed so shrewd and confident. Or perhaps Henry's own guilt made him suspicious. For whatever reason, Henry did not altogether trust Mary's obedient submission. One day, when he thought he had won her trust through his gifts and kindness, he called her to him and, on his own with her, asked her to tell him how she really felt. He hated lying, he told her. He would rather know the truth. She could tell him in the strictest confidence.

It must have been a tricky moment for Mary, who really did hate lying, but fortunately she had enough sense not to fall into her father's trap. She told him that she had meant every word of what she had said. In that case, said Henry, she wouldn't mind writing to Charles V and the pope to tell them that she really had changed her mind, of her own free will, about the legality of her mother's marriage and her own legitimacy. Mary had little choice. She did as he asked, but this time, too, she sent other, secret messages to her relatives that said exactly the opposite.

Henry wasn't just trying to trap Mary for the sake of it. In the years since he had divorced Queen Catherine, Henry's policies meant that England had become increasingly isolated from other European countries. By getting Mary to sign and to stand by her submission, Henry was sending a message to her European relatives, telling them there was no longer a dispute between him and Mary.

In fact, the rift between father and daughter was deeper than ever. As head of the Church, Henry had decided to get rid of all the monasteries and convents in England. Henry pretended that this was because monks and nuns no longer lived according to the vows they had taken — vows of poverty (to own nothing), chastity (not to marry or have relationships), and obedience (to obey Church law). In this, he was partly right. Although some monks and nuns had a strong inner calling to dedicate their lives to God, some did not. Many were younger sons and daughters of rich families who lived in religious orders but behaved as if they didn't. Of course, this wasn't Henry's real reason for wanting to close down the monasteries and convents. The real reason was that many religious orders were very wealthy. Down the centuries people had made big donations of land and other property. And Henry was broke.

In 1535, his chief minister, Cromwell, organized a list of the value of all church property. There was a lot of it, and it would solve all Henry's money worries. Over the next couple of years, the smaller monasteries were attacked first. The monks and nuns were thrown out, the property belonging to their order was seized, and the buildings were either razed to the ground or sold and put to a different use. Elizabeth was given a former monastery as a palace, and many nobles bought or were awarded Church property. This was a clever move on Henry's part, because it meant that these people now had a vested interest in the property — they would not want it returned to the Church.

However, there were now hundred of monks and nuns with nowhere to live and no means of earning a living. This situation caused a wave of resentment against Henry across Catholic Europe. It also meant that, for the first time, ordinary people — as opposed to courtiers and politicians — were seeing what it meant to have the king, rather than the pope, running the religious life of the country, and many of them didn't like it. Henry was in for the most worrisome time of his life as riots broke out in different parts of the country.

Some of these riots were more about poor harvests and hunger than religion, but in Yorkshire one of the biggest uprisings was led by a one-eyed lawyer, Robert Aske. He called his rebellion the Pilgrimage of Grace, and he demanded that the pope's authority be restored, the Church be returned to its former power, and that Mary be declared the legitimate daughter of the king.

For Henry, this was like a red flag to a bull. He sent the Duke of Norfolk to Yorkshire to deal with Aske. Norfolk promised Aske and his followers a pardon if they went peacefully. Aske agreed. Later, he was hanged for his pains, along with all the other protesters and some monks from a newly restored abbey. The policy of closing the monasteries was speeded up. As the bigger and wealthier establishments were closed down, the earls who had saved Henry's kingdom for him were rewarded. The Earl of Shrewsbury received five abbeys and two priories, and the Earl of Rutland received six abbeys. All in all, the "Dissolution of the Monasteries," as it became known, is believed to have brought Henry one and a half million pounds, which would be billions and billions of dollars in today's money. But it also made him very unpopular. "Old Harry" became another name for the devil in the parts of the country where rebellions had been cruelly put down.

As for Mary, it was a source of real grief to her that so many beautiful statues were destroyed and so many abbeys and monasteries passed into private hands. She felt for the monks and nuns who were cast out to make their way in an unfriendly world. Of course, she did not dare voice any of her feelings to her father. To do so would have been extremely dangerous. Instead, she played the dutiful daughter, grateful to be welcome at court, and kept her opinions to herself.

Thanks to the birth of Edward, the succession to the

English throne was clear and undisputed for the first time in Henry's reign. Henry Fitzroy had died of tuberculosis in 1536. Edward was now the only son — and he was legitimate. For a few brief years, Mary and Elizabeth were not rivals for the crown. Now that she no longer saw her sister as a threat, Mary seems to have grown quite fond of Elizabeth, telling her father she was a "toward" child (meaning she was very advanced for her age) and that one day he would be very proud of her. Mary was very musical, and she taught Elizabeth to play the lute and virginals and gave her presents of jewelry.

But was Mary genuinely fond of Elizabeth at the time, or was she just keeping on the safe side of her father? No one has ever been able to decide.

WHEN QUEEN JANE DIED, Elizabeth was still only four years old, but she was an extremely intelligent child; even if she didn't understand everything that was going on around her, she knew that the arrival of her new brother had made things better in some ways (her father now had what he had always wanted) and worse in others (in getting it, he had lost his wife).

It is not known how soon Elizabeth became aware of the religious differences in the way she and Mary were brought up. Mary had had a thoroughly Catholic education. Elizabeth's education was in the hands of religious reformists, starting with Kat Ashley, Elizabeth's governess, who had taken over from Lady Bryan when Edward was born. Kat was a highly educated woman, and she taught Elizabeth an impressive range of subjects, including arithmetic, reading, history, geography, astronomy, architecture, and a smattering of Italian, French, Spanish, and Flemish. (Flemish was important in those days because the Low Countries, now known as Holland and Belgium, formed the central part of the Holy Roman Empire.) As if that wasn't enough, Kat also taught Elizabeth needlework, dancing, and riding.

Unlike Mary's childhood, Elizabeth's was not a long series of betrothals to powerful foreign suitors. In fact, nobody much wanted to marry Elizabeth, whose own father had declared her illegitimate and whose mother had been executed for adultery. She seldom went to court, because Henry did not like to be reminded of her mother. This meant that Elizabeth grew up quietly in her various palaces in the countryside around what is now the outskirts of London.

Over the next twelve years, Elizabeth and Edward would have three more stepmothers. The first of these Henry chose more or less by mail order. There were no photographs in those days, so he sent Hans Holbein, a famous portrait painter, around Europe to paint royal women Henry thought it might be politically useful to marry. When Holbein came back, he brought with him a collection of miniature portraits. Henry is said to have asked Elizabeth which of the royal candidates she thought he should marry. Very diplomatically, Elizabeth — still only five — told him he should choose the one he liked best.

Henry settled on the German princess Anne of Cleves, but when he saw her in real life, on the eve of their wedding in 1540, he was furious. In his opinion, she looked nothing like her portrait. (She seems to have been a homely woman, not nearly as well educated or sophisticated as his other wives.) Although Henry went through with the wedding, he was deeply depressed at the idea of remaining married to Anne. She was persuaded to allow the marriage to be annulled. Poor Anne did not want to return home a rejected bride, so she spent the rest of her life in England as a sort of royal aunt, riding beside Elizabeth in processions and teaching her embroidery.

The same year brought Elizabeth her next stepmother. This one could not have been more different from Anne of Cleves. She was Catherine Howard, a cousin of Anne Boleyn — English, young, pretty, and extremely flighty. As first cousin once removed to the new queen, Elizabeth was given a place of honor at the wedding banquet.

But this marriage was doomed from the start. Henry by this time was nearly 50, and Catherine was only 16. She also had a boyfriend whom she much preferred to Henry. Any sensible girl would have given up the boyfriend on her marriage. Not Catherine. She continued to play around, with him and others, scandalizing courtiers, until finally she was caught. Henry did not take kindly to being betrayed in this way. This time it was not a case of made-up charges, as it had been with Anne Boleyn. Catherine really had committed adultery. She was tried and executed, along with several partners in crime.

Elizabeth was devastated. She had liked Catherine, who had seemed more like an older sister than a stepmother. Even if Elizabeth had no conscious memory of what had happened to her mother, Catherine's execution must have made it very real for her and brought home the horror of it.

In July 1543, when Elizabeth was ten, Henry married for the last time. His latest choice was the still young but twice widowed Catherine Parr. Catherine did not really want to marry Henry — and who can blame her? Quite apart from the fact that marriage to Henry seriously threatened a woman's life, he was no longer attractive. By this time he was vastly overweight, short of breath, and suffering from painful, stinking, infected ulcers on both legs, for which he used many salves and potions, including a paste of powdered pearls. And there was another reason, too. Both Catherine's previous husbands had been older men, and until Henry lumbered into her life, she had been hoping to marry for love. The man she wished to marry was Thomas Seymour, brother of Jane Seymour and uncle of Prince Edward.

Marrying the king might have seemed a shortcut to the grave, but turning him down would have been an even shorter one. Catherine did not dare say no. Thomas Seymour removed himself from the scene the moment Henry declared his intentions. For the rest of Henry's life, Catherine concentrated on being a loyal wife and a good stepmother to Elizabeth and Edward. It was thanks to Catherine that the two younger royals were taught by a group of reformist scholars from Oxford and Cambridge. Elizabeth did so well that she was given her own tutor, William Grindal. He drove her very hard, which worried another tutor, Roger Ascham. He wrote to Kat Ashley, telling her to make sure that Elizabeth didn't overdo it:

> If you pour much drink at once into a goblet, the most part will dash out and run over. If ye pour it softly, you may fill it even to the top, and so Her Grace, I doubt not, by little and little may be increased in learning.

Elizabeth, however, loved learning. She studied the Bible every day in Greek. She translated classical texts from Latin and Greek into English and back again. As well as French, Italian, and Spanish, she spoke Latin. In fact, she spoke it so fluently that when she was queen she was able to lose her temper in Latin with a foreign ambassador. Roger Ascham wrote about her:

> Her mind has no womanly weakness, her perseverance is equal to that of a man, and her memory long keeps what it quickly picks up.

Being smart was also a way of getting attention and love. For Christmas 1545, when she was 12, Elizabeth excelled herself. She translated a small book written by Catherine Parr into three languages, Latin, French, and

Italian, then embroidered a red cover for the translations with gold and silver threads and sent it as a present to her father.

Henry was pleased with the present and proud of his daughter. She was invited to court more often now, together with Mary and Edward. Though she and Mary were both still technically illegitimate, Henry treated them as his daughters. But for Elizabeth, there was always the worry that she was less legitimate than Mary. There were plenty of people at court who remembered Mary's mother and her own. Many people still thought Henry had done wrong by Catherine and Mary and whispered that while Mary had been born in wedlock, whatever Henry said, Elizabeth most definitely had not. Perhaps this was why Elizabeth, as she grew up, gained a reputation for arrogance. Jane Dormer, who would later become one of Mary's ladies-in-waiting, called her "proud and disdainful." Like many others, she thought Elizabeth had inherited this trait from Anne Boleyn, along with a liking for flirtation. So even when things were as good as they could get for Elizabeth, there was always a big question mark hanging over her future. Had she inherited her mother's bad blood? And indeed, her mother being the wicked woman she was, was she even Henry's daughter?

No wonder Elizabeth held her head high and seemed proud and disdainful. Who wouldn't, with rumors like that being whispered behind her back?

Mary
The Dutiful Daughter
1537 – 1546

POOR MARY. As she watched her father marrying time after time, did she remember all her own childhood betrothals that had promised a glittering future as the consort of one of Europe's leading kings? Now it seemed there would never be any prospect of marriage for her. Twenty-one when Henry married Jane Seymour, Mary was 30 when he married Catherine Parr. At a time when princesses married at 14, Mary was definitely on the shelf.

Throughout all this period, Mary was treated as a leading lady of the court. In the intervals when Henry was not married, she was *the* leading lady. She led the mourners at Jane Seymour's funeral and became like a mother to the orphaned baby Edward. When Anne of Cleves arrived in England to marry Henry, Mary was at the dock to greet her. Mary didn't approve of Henry's fifth wife — Catherine Howard was too young, too flirtatious, *and* from the same ambitious family as Anne Boleyn. When Catherine's affairs were discovered, Mary was put in charge of Elizabeth and Edward, who were sent away to protect them from gossip and scandal. Mary must have been aware how deeply disturbed Elizabeth was by Catherine Howard's death.

By the time Mary's father married Catherine Parr, he had become so fond of Mary again that he and his new wife took her with them on their honeymoon, perhaps as a companion for Catherine (the two women were nearly the same age). Mary became ill and went back. She spent the rest of the year with her brother and sister. When she next came to court, Henry had increased her status. He had not restored her to the rank of princess (that would have been too close to admitting he might have made a mistake or two in the past), but he had restored her to the succession. Under the Act of Succession passed in 1544, Edward was to become king when Henry died. If he died without heirs, then Mary would become queen of England. If both Edward and Mary died without children, then Elizabeth would succeed to the throne. And because Henry was realistic enough to know that he was unlikely to live a long life, he began putting plans in place for a Council of Regency that would rule until Edward became an adult.

At the same time, Henry promised Mary that he would find her a husband, but Mary guessed that he was not looking very hard. She knew that if he married her to a foreign prince, that prince might invade England to put her on the throne; and if he married her to an Englishman, then it would increase the risk of civil war. And so Mary, who had always longed to marry and have children, remained an old maid at court.

Among Mary's supporters, there was general agreement about who would make her a good husband. He was an Englishman and a Catholic named Reginald Pole, son of Mary's loyal godmother and governess, Margaret Pole. As a young man, he had been a great favorite of Henry's. The king had sent Pole on a tour of the Catholic courts of Europe to drum up support for his divorce from Catherine of Aragon. When he came back, Henry offered to make him Bishop of York, but Pole guessed what lay ahead. He knew that Henry was planning to break away from the Church of Rome and that he would be expected to play along. Not wanting to do this, he fled the country. Later, he wrote a paper attacking Henry's religious policy, which, given the fact that his family still lived in England, was not very wise. Later still, the pope made him a cardinal and sent him to Flanders to do what he could to help the rebels in Yorkshire.

From Henry's point of view, Reginald Pole was a traitor. He was also dangerous for another reason. He had a possible claim to the English throne. Henry was always wary of such people because his own claim did not go back very far. He was only the second Tudor to be king of England. His father, Henry VII, had won the final battle of the Wars of the Roses between rival families, the Yorkists and Lancastrians. It is said that he had literally *found* the crown of England hanging on a bush in the middle of the Battle of Bosworth, grabbed it, and put it on his own head.

Henry VII was a Lancastrian. Pole was descended from the Yorkist side. Married to Mary, his claim to the throne would be strengthened. So when Henry heard what he was up to in Flanders, he had Pole's younger brother, Geoffrey, arrested and threatened with torture. Geoffrey caved in and told Henry's examiners all the rude things that different members of his family had said about Henry — and that the possibility of Reginald's marriage to Mary had been discussed.

Immediately, all the other members of the family were rounded up and imprisoned. Their houses were searched, including the house of Reginald's now elderly mother, Margaret. In Margaret's house a design for a new coat of arms was found. It had pansies (the Poles' family emblem) intertwined with marigolds (to represent Mary), and growing out from among them was the tree of true Catholic faith.

That was enough for Henry. To him, this was treason. Reginald's eldest brother, Henry Lord Montague, was arrested and executed, along with a cousin, Henry Courtenay, Marquess of Exeter. Montague's young son was sent to the Tower and disappeared without a trace. Exeter's wife and son, Edward Courtenay, were also sent to the Tower. Margaret Pole was sentenced to death, too. The sentence hung over her for two years. She was beheaded in 1541, at age 69. On the scaffold she asked the bystanders to pray for the king, for Prince Edward, and "Princess Mary." It was the first time anyone had called Mary "princess" in public for many years, but Margaret Pole had nothing to lose.

Mary, on the other hand, had lost another mother. It must have been very hard to bear.

Mary did not dare show her feelings about any of this. Instead, she played the role of dutiful daughter, helping to nurse her father alongside Catherine Parr, his loyal wife. The two women were close friends, despite the fact that they had different religious beliefs. Mary remained a devout Catholic, grieving for the lost abbeys and monasteries of England, while Catherine was more Protestant than Henry, who had only ever been anti-Catholic when it suited him.

In fact, Henry had always persecuted people he thought too Protestant, and by the end of his reign, he was burning them at the stake. At one stage, it looked as if Henry would have Catherine's head. She only got out of trouble by falling on her knees, telling him she was just an idiotic woman, and begging him to set her straight. Perhaps it was because neither Catherine nor Mary dared discuss their true beliefs for fear of Henry that Mary and her last stepmother were able to remain so close during Henry's lifetime.

To visiting ambassadors, life at the royal court seemed calm and tranquil. The king kept more and more to his own quarters, nursing his ulcers. The queen and Mary entertained foreign dignitaries. The unhappiness that either of them may have felt was not apparent. One of the last entries in the accounts of Henry's reign was the price of a horse — "a white-grey gelding" — for Mary.

In late January 1547, Henry VIII died at Whitehall Palace. Mary was in the palace when he died, but she was not officially told of his death for several days. Along with many of Henry's councillors, she was kept in the dark. The reason was simple. The Council of Regency, set up to rule the country until nine-year-old Edward came of age, was strongly Protestant. And the Council did not want any trouble from Catholic Mary or her supporters.

Like Mother, Like Daughter?

FOR THE LAST eight years of Henry's reign, the rivalry between Mary and Elizabeth died down. The reason was simple. Henry had a male heir, and provided nothing untoward happened to Edward, neither sister would inherit the crown. For Elizabeth especially, it now must have seemed a distant prospect.

Then, at the end of January 1547, everything changed. Elizabeth was at her lessons when there was an unexpected interruption. Her brother had come to see her. With him was his uncle, Edward Seymour, Earl of Hertford. This was very unusual. The royal children weren't in the habit of dropping in on one another. At this stage, Edward didn't know what it was about, either.

Edward Seymour had brought the two children together because he had something important to tell them and he wanted them to hear it together. Henry, the father they loved and dreaded, had died. Elizabeth and Edward, his two Protestant children, were scared by the news. They clung to each other and burst into tears. When they calmed down, both knew that things would be different between them. They were no longer simply brother and sister. Edward was king of England and Elizabeth was still only Lady Elizabeth. From now on, Elizabeth must kneel when she came into Edward's presence. When they dined together, she would have to sit so that the Cloth of State, the canopy over the king's seat, did not hang over her. And she must always sit at a lower level than the king, so that meant a low bench or a cushion on the floor.

The next day, Edward was taken to London for his father's funeral. The procession following the enormous coffin was four miles long. A month later, he was crowned. Women did not usually attend the funerals of men (just as men did not attend the funerals of women), but Elizabeth was not invited to her brother's coronation, either. This was a pity, for probably she would have liked to see her brother in his coronation finery. Edward wore cloth of silver and a white velvet cloak, and he rode a horse with crimson trappings embroidered with gold and pearls. One of his favorite moments came on the eve of his coronation, when a tightrope walker from Aragon plunged down a rope from the top of a church steeple to the ground. Edward laughed with excitement and wanted to stay for more.

Although well-wishers called him "the young Solomon," after King Solomon in the Bible who was the wisest of kings, Edward was not yet old enough to rule. Henry knew this and had left instructions for a Council of Regency to govern England. Secretly, his uncle, Edward Seymour, had altered these instructions to make himself the most important member of the Council and Lord Protector of England.

Henry had left Elizabeth well provided for, with an income of £3,000 a year and a dowry of £10,000 when she married, provided she had the consent of the Council of Regency. (If she didn't, there would be no dowry.) Catherine Parr had also been left comfortably off, and it was agreed that Elizabeth would live with her. The two of them moved into Chelsea Palace on the Thames River in London, where Elizabeth was to continue her education. It should have been the quiet, respectable life of a Protestant gentlewoman.

Unfortunately for Elizabeth, there was someone else on the scene: Thomas Seymour, Admiral of England and brother of the new Lord Protector. Thomas was 38 years old, handsome, charming, and very ambitious. Thomas was angry with his brother because he thought they should have shared power equally between them. Instead, Edward Seymour was now the most powerful man in England. He even had a new title to go with it — Duke of Somerset. Admiral Thomas wanted to overthrow him and was prepared to do whatever it took to do it.

Thomas's first plan was to marry Elizabeth. The Council of Regency said no. So he decided to woo Catherine Parr, with whom his love affair had been so rudely interrupted by Henry VIII. It's not clear if Catherine knew she was not his first choice, but if she did, she would probably have forgiven him. She was very much in love with him. He visited Chelsea Palace a lot, but secretly, for he knew that the Council of Regency would have an opinion on this relationship, too. It was not proper for a dowager queen (a king's widow) to remarry until a decent interval of mourning had passed. Catherine suggested they wait two years, knowing in her heart that Thomas was unlikely to wait for her that long. By April 1547, only three months after Henry's death, there were rumors of a secret marriage and of a gate left unlocked to allow Thomas to visit Chelsea Palace in the middle of the night.

How much did Elizabeth know of this? We simply don't know. She was probably not told about night visits, but she may have heard the servants gossiping and she probably saw Seymour when he came visiting during the day. However, the fact that Catherine was effectively Elizabeth's guardian may have contributed to Catherine's anxiety about being found out. At any rate, in May 1547, she went to her stepson, King Edward, and told him privately that she had married Thomas Seymour. Edward, who loved his stepmother, promised not to tell his other uncle, whom he was beginning to dislike intensely.

This was exactly the sort of game Thomas Seymour enjoyed. He had gotten the better of his brother. The king was on his side, and Thomas made sure he stayed that way. He learned from a servant of the king's bedchamber that Edward was kept short of pocket money, and he fixed that. Not surprisingly, Edward came to prefer jolly Uncle Thomas to mean Uncle Edward. And when Thomas's scandalous marriage was discovered in June, he wrote to him and to Catherine, promising:

> I will provide for you both that if any grief befall, I shall be a sufficient succour [comfort] in your godly or praisable enterprises.

The Lord Protector could hardly quarrel publicly with the king about this. Thomas Seymour had gotten away with it. He was married to the old king's widow and was effectively stepfather to the second in line to the throne.

Thomas Seymour was tall, handsome, good fun, and a tremendous flirt — a bit like Henry VIII, in fact (before he became fat and bad tempered). It wasn't surprising that, before long, 14-year-old Elizabeth developed a huge crush on him. What was much more puzzling was why Catherine Parr allowed him to act as he did. He used to come into Elizabeth's bedroom in the early mornings, before she was up, and tickle her. Elizabeth began to get up earlier and earlier so that he would find her dressed and at her studies. Kat Ashley, Elizabeth's governess of many years, complained to Catherine Parr. Catherine then started coming with him and joining in the horseplay. One time, when they were fooling about in the garden, she held Elizabeth while her husband cut her dress to shreds.

Elizabeth clearly had mixed feelings about all this. On the one hand, she was afraid of what people would say. On the other, it must have been flattering to have such a handsome, dashing man find her attractive. Things came to a head when Catherine, by this time pregnant, walked in to find her husband kissing Elizabeth. She did not want a public scandal, but she didn't want the girl under her roof anymore.

Almost a year after Catherine's secret marriage, Elizabeth was sent to live with Sir Antony and Lady Denny at Cheshunt in Hertfordshire. She was sorry she had hurt Catherine and wrote her letters apologizing and wishing her well with the birth of her baby.

Catherine Parr died just days after the birth of her daughter in August 1548. Elizabeth had been ill all summer, perhaps as a result of the upset with Catherine, perhaps because she was missing Thomas. With little thought that Elizabeth had loved Catherine, an excited Kat Ashley came to her sickroom and said, "Your old husband that was appointed to you after the death of the King is free again. You may have him if you will."

There was a long silence, then Elizabeth said, "No."

Kat Ashley wasn't fooled. She knew Elizabeth was still in love with Thomas. "Yes," Kat said, "if my Lord Protector and the Council were pleased therewith."

Elizabeth still said no and refused Kat's suggestion that she should write a letter of condolence to Seymour. She didn't believe a man who had behaved as he had could have truly loved his wife.

In fact, he had loved her and he missed her a good deal. But Seymour was a man of the world. Now that Queen Catherine was dead, he plotted openly to overthrow his brother. He asked various other noblemen to support him, he rode down to the West Country to make sure the Navy would come in on his side, and he still had his eye on Elizabeth. He had already discussed Elizabeth's finances with her cofferer, or treasurer, Thomas Parry.

People were beginning to notice what Thomas Seymour was up to. One day, as they rode in procession, Lord Russell, a senior member of the King's Council, took him to task. He asked Seymour how he thought he was going to live on Elizabeth's dowry. Thomas gaily replied that they would also have her £3,000 a year allowance. Lord Russell was furious and told Seymour that he personally, as a member of the Council, would not consent to the marriage. Seymour took no notice. He wrote to Elizabeth, suggesting marriage. Wisely, Elizabeth did not reply.

It does seem that Kat Ashley was right. Elizabeth was in love, for she then found an excuse to write to him. She wanted to spend Christmas in London and wrote asking if he knew anywhere she could stay. Elizabeth was duly invited to make use of Chelsea Palace, the house in which she had lived with Seymour and Catherine after her father's death. That same December, Kat Ashley found herself written off by the Duchess of Somerset for allowing Elizabeth to go on the river with Thomas Seymour without a guardian.

Meanwhile, Thomas Seymour planned to overthrow his brother, the Duke of Somerset, by force. He had discovered that the vice treasurer of the Bristol Mint was shaving gold from newly minted coins, and instead of turning him in, he blackmailed him for a share of the gold to pay for his own fighting men. Thomas copied the keys to the young king's private garden with a view to kidnapping him. In case young Edward refused to cooperate once kidnapped, he made a stamp of the king's signature. He stockpiled arms at his house at Sudeley, and he bragged to everyone about how well his plans were going. Elizabeth's treasurer, Thomas Parry, heard rumors of some of this and came back to Hatfield to tell Kat Ashley that he didn't think Thomas Seymour was the right man for Elizabeth, but Kat Ashley dismissed his concerns.

In January 1549, the Duke of Somerset warned his brother that he knew what he was up to. Thomas Seymour took no notice. Instead, he moved ahead with his plan to kidnap King Edward. Using his forged key, he led a band of armed men into the king's room at

Hampton Court. They roused Edward's dog, a spaniel. It barked and came rushing at him, and to the young king's horror, Thomas Seymour shot it dead with his pistol. By this time the noise had alerted the guards. Seymour had the nerve to tell them that he was just testing the security around the king.

Four days later, on January 20, 1548, Sir Antony Denny (Elizabeth's host when she was banished by Catherine Parr) and Sir Robert Tyrwhit arrived at Hatfield House demanding to speak to Elizabeth. Thomas Seymour was in the Tower of London, accused of plotting against his brother. The Duke of Somerset was also convinced that Thomas had been planning another secret marriage, this time to Elizabeth. The question was, had Elizabeth been planning it with him?

Tyrwhit was under orders to get enough evidence to convict Thomas Seymour. The first thing he did was send Thomas Parry and Kat Ashley to the Tower. Then he began to interrogate a tearful and frightened Elizabeth. She did not know what her servants might be saying, and Tyrwhit wouldn't tell her. Over the next few days, she admitted that the possibility of marriage had been discussed and that Thomas Seymour had agreed to lend her his house for a few days. Her servants said much the same thing at first. Then Kat Ashley was put in a deep, dark, cold dungeon to encourage her to talk. She stuck to her story, but Thomas Parry, scared that the same or worse would happen to him, began to spill the beans. He told how Elizabeth had been caught kissing Thomas

Seymour when she was 14, how she still hankered after him, and how marriage had been discussed.

Kat Ashley was shown his written confession. Cursing Parry, she agreed that it was true and that she and Elizabeth had often discussed marriage, but never, she insisted, had they considered going behind the back of the Council.

Now Elizabeth was confronted with both confessions. She was "much abashed and half-breathless," according to Tyrwhit, but she was also clever enough to know that she could not be convicted of treason simply for finding Seymour attractive. Nor had her servants committed treason.

Nevertheless, Tyrwhit kept bullying her, certain that there was more to this business than Elizabeth admitted. Elizabeth held firm, writing to the Lord Protector, apologizing, and explaining her position. Somerset was content with this. He had enough evidence to execute his brother. But Kat Ashley and Thomas Parry were not allowed to return to her service. Instead, Lady Tyrwhit took over as Elizabeth's "lady governess." Elizabeth was deeply upset. Kat Ashley had been with her since she was six years old. Elizabeth wept and sulked. She hated Lady Tyrwhit and wrote to the Lord Protector, saying "people will say through my lewd demeanour I deserved to have such a one." The Lord Protector wrote back warning her not to be brash.

Kat Ashley and Thomas Parry remained in prison. Thomas Seymour was charged with treason. He asked to be tried in open court, but the Council decided to avoid a trial by passing an Act of Parliament sentencing him to death. By March 8, 1549, the news had reached Hatfield, where Tyrwhit reported that Elizabeth "began a little to droop." He also said that she had started to defend him whenever she heard people criticizing him. On March 20, Seymour was executed on Tower Hill. When Elizabeth was told of his death, she is supposed to have said, "This day died a man of much wit and little judgement."

But Thomas Seymour's death cut her to the quick. It was the third time in her short life that someone she deeply cared about had been beheaded. Once again, the reason was connected with love and marriage.

"What Is to Become of Me?"
Mary
1547 – 1552

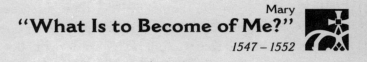

MARY WAS NOT SURPRISED when stories reached her about Elizabeth. In her opinion, Elizabeth was already far too flirtatious. She had never felt that Chelsea Palace, with its scandalous goings-on, was the right place for an impressionable 14-year-old. (She had also heard the rumors about Catherine Parr and Thomas Seymour.) Mary had written to Elizabeth at the start of Edward's reign, offering her a home, but Elizabeth had refused.

Throughout this period, Mary lived on her estates in the country and observed a long period of mourning for her father. She was upset by many things that had happened since her father died. In the first place, Edward Seymour had made sure she was the last to learn of her father's death. Mary knew why. He and his Council were all strong Protestants. They wanted no interference from Catholic Mary and her friends.

Mary must have known that this was likely to happen. Although she had always been very close to Edward — according to one of her ladies-in-waiting, he had taken "special content in her company" — they disagreed strongly on religion. Even before he came to the throne, Edward had started to try to put his big sister right about the way she lived her life. When she was 30 and he was eight years old, he wrote her a letter of advice: "Foreign dances and merriments do not become a most Christian princess," he told her, advising her to cut them out. Edward was turning into the sort of Protestant who thought that bright colors, jewelry, music, and dancing were Catholic and therefore bad.

Once he was King, Edward became even more aggressively anti-Catholic. In this he was fully supported by Somerset and the Council. Their agenda was to push a series of religious reforms through Parliament, one of the most famous of which was called the Act of Uniformity. Under this Act, the Latin Bible and Latin mass, favored by Catholics, were banned. In the future, services would be in English and prayers taken from the Book of Common Prayer. The clergy were to be allowed to marry. And statues of Jesus, the Virgin Mary, and the saints were forbidden. So were lots of other Catholic traditions, such as celebrating saints' days and lighting candles for people when you prayed for them. Mary was outraged. Her religion was under attack and she began to fight back.

In March 1549, on same day that Parliament passed the Act of Uniformity, Mary ordered a special mass and announced that from now on there would be three masses a day in her house and that local people were invited to come. But she knew she was not going to get away with that for long.

All her life Mary had looked to Spain and the Holy Roman Empire for help and support. Charles V was her cousin, after all. So when she found herself seated next to his Imperial Ambassador Francis Van der Delft at the christening of one of the children of John Dudley, the Earl of Warwick, she told him how worried she was about her future and begged him to speak to the Duke of Somerset on her behalf.

Somerset wasn't eager to give Mary permission to hear mass. She was heir to the throne, after all, and it wasn't exactly presenting a united front if the king decreed one thing and his heir did another. But Van der Delft kept at him, explaining that all Mary wanted was permission to go on practicing her Catholicism until her brother came of age. At present, she felt he was too young to make up his mind about religion. Somerset had other things on his mind — the execution of his own brother had made him unpopular, and there were disturbances springing up across the country. So he said yes, off the record, without telling the other members of the Council. In fact, the agreement was worthless — Somerset was losing his power by the day.

The Act of Uniformity was due to take effect on Whitsunday (Pentecost) 1549. Two days before, two messengers from the Council rode up to Mary's door.

They told her that she was subject to the new law like anyone else in the land. Henceforth, the hearing of mass was to cease. Mary stood her ground and told them that they had altered her father's religious settlement and that she did not recognize the new law.

Mary was not alone in resisting. That Whitsuntide, in Cornwall, villagers were so offended by the new service in English that they forced their priest to celebrate mass the next day. Soon people all over the West Country were demanding the return of their statues of the Virgin and the saints. There were uprisings in Oxfordshire, Gloucestershire, and Hertfordshire. The biggest rebellion was in Norfolk, where 30,000 people gathered behind a local lawyer named Robert Ket. But this was not a Catholic rebellion, it was about land and money. For years now, landowners had been enclosing common land to graze their large flocks of sheep, leaving the commoners with nowhere to graze their household animals. Thousands of people had been put out of their home and had become beggars. Inflation was high, and Ket wanted economic reform.

All these uprisings were the beginning of the end for the Duke of Somerset. He had lost control of the country. The Council could see civil war looming.

Mary took no part in the rebellions, although she must have been tempted. But at a time like this, her very existence posed a threat to the Council. Members of the Council started saying that Mary was the channel by which "the rats of Rome" might return and overrun their

Protestant stronghold. They talked about the Catholic nobility as the "Marian Faction." They feared that one of Mary's friends, at home or abroad, might assassinate Edward so that Mary could be queen. In turn, Mary feared that she would be killed to stop her from getting in the way of the Protestant revolution.

The man who brought order to the country was John Dudley, Earl of Warwick (later Duke of Northumberland). Dudley was the best military leader in the country. He was also a cunning and ruthless man. After bringing the Ket rebellion to an end, he took control as leader of the Council. He was every bit as determined as Somerset had been to see the Protestant reforms go through. And he was no friend of Mary's. It was fear of what the future might hold for her under Dudley that led Mary to panic. She decided to flee the country.

On a foggy night in July 1550, a Flemish ship sailed up an estuary in Essex called the Blackwater and docked at the port of Maldon. It carried a cargo of grain destined for Lady Mary, heir to the throne of England, who was staying at a nearby house called Woodham Walter.

But the ship was not what it seemed — and neither was the captain. This was a rescue mission to smuggle Mary out of England. The captain was Jean Dubois, the secretary of the former imperial ambassador, Francis Van der Delft. Beyond the Blackwater, out at sea, sailed eight more Flemish ships, supposedly on the lookout for

Scottish pirates sheltering in English waters. They were really there to protect the rescue.

The plan was that Mary would be ready to leave the next day, but when Dubois arrived, Mary had not even begun to pack. Instead, one of her servants, the controller of her household, Sir Robert Rochester, wanted to meet Dubois. The two men met in a lonely churchyard in the dead of night. This was very dangerous for Dubois. If they had been seen, he would have been arrested right away.

Dubois could not figure out what was going on. Rochester seemed to be against the escape. He said Mary's household was "not so free of enemies of her religion as she imagined," and that she would never make it past the guards. He asked Dubois to come to see Mary.

Dubois was extremely reluctant. This was not what they had arranged. The plan had been that Mary would be brought to the boat and they would sail immediately. Now he was being asked to hang around and go to visit the woman whom the Council feared most. Yet Dubois knew how badly Mary had wanted to leave the country just the previous month, and he did not want to abandon her unless she herself told him that she did not want to go. So, very nervous, he spent the next day thinking up excuses to delay the grain deal, and the next evening he visited Mary.

Dubois found Mary confused. She was now half packed but couldn't decide whether to go or not. Was it fear of being caught? Or had she received some new information that made her reluctant to leave? During their interview, Rochester reminded her that an astrologer had predicted that her brother would be dead within the year. What would happen to her claim to the throne if she was not in the country? Then he left the room and came back shortly afterward with the news that things had taken a turn for the worse. He said that the sheriff at Maldon suspected something and that there were two English warships in the estuary. They had spotted the Flemish warships out at sea and thought there was a plot afoot. The sheriff was going to impound Dubois's boat. Worse, he was putting guards everywhere — even in the church tower, which had a clear view of the estuary and the countryside for miles around.

Dubois knew it was now impossible for Mary to leave. He was doubtful that even he would be able to get away safely.

Mary became very frightened. Her rescue cut off, she began weeping, "What is to become of me?" Dubois knew that the only thing he could do for her now was get clear of the house before they were all caught red-handed. Rochester recruited a local man to lead him back to Maldon by a back road through the woods. It was midnight when they got there. The town was quiet and the guards were civil, but they wanted a bribe to let Dubois pass. Dubois's escort said they could have Mary's grain.

Dubois caught the high tide and sailed that night. But there were no warships in the Channel, and as his boat passed the church tower, there was not a guard in sight. A storm blew up as he reached the open sea, and he and the rest of the Flemish fleet were storm bound for days. No English warships came to challenge them. Either the Council had no idea that Mary had been trying to escape or they knew very well that she had not gone.

From this story it seems clear that Rochester was the one who didn't want Mary to leave. Afterward, he behaved as a loyal servant to her, so perhaps he genuinely believed it was not in her best interest.

As for the Council, they may have had wind of Mary's escape even before it had been attempted. If not, they certainly heard about it afterward. Enough English townspeople and Flemish sailors had guessed what was going on, and rumors started flying. Soon people were gossiping the length and breadth of Europe. Mary had fled England, they said. She was now living under the protection of the Holy Roman Emperor's sister, the Regent of Flanders.

The Council in England was embarrassed and annoyed. Members of the Council put out some propaganda of their own — that the Holy Roman Emperor had made a disgraceful attempt to kidnap Lady Mary against her will but had been foiled just in time. Perhaps because they wanted to stop the rumors, they wanted Mary to appear in public. Edward invited her to come to court for Christmas 1550. For the first time since Edward had come to the throne, he and his two sisters spent the Christmas season together.

That Christmas didn't go well. Mary was irritated that she was not given a royal escort. Edward challenged her about having mass celebrated at her house. Mary told him he was far too young to be telling her what to do. When she burst into tears, he cried, too, and told her it didn't matter. But they weren't getting along, and Mary left before the most important date of the royal year: Twelfth Night, the only night of the year when the king wore his crown. She did not want to watch Elizabeth being top sister at court. In Mary's opinion, Elizabeth had been restored to favor far too soon after the Seymour affair.

Not long afterward, Mary received a stern letter from her brother. In it she was ordered to stop holding mass and to use the Protestant service instead. Most of the letter had been written by the Council, but the last paragraph had been written by Edward himself:

> *I say this with certain intention, I will see my laws strictly obeyed and those who break them will be watched and denounced.*

Mary was summoned to court to give her reaction.

Mary returned to London. This time, she arrived like a mighty princess. She was escorted by 130 gentlemen and ladies of her household, all dressed in her colors, blue and yellow. As a challenge to the Council, all openly wore Catholic crosses and rosaries. They rode from Essex like a small army, and as they did so, people from the local villages lined the route, some of them running as much as five miles to see and greet Mary. When she reached London, her procession could hardly get through the streets as more people joined her and others crowded to see her.

The Council didn't like this display of power and popularity. Mary was separated from all her supporters and taken in to see her brother. This time the two had a tremendous argument that went on for two hours. Neither Edward nor Mary would budge. At the end, Mary stated the truth as she saw it:

> There are only two things: soul and body. My soul I offer to God, and my body to Your Majesty's service, and so may it please you to take away my life rather than the old religion in which I desire to live and die.

Once again, Edward crumbled. He sent Mary back home, with no agreement that she would give up the mass. Next day, via the imperial ambassador, came a threat from the Holy Roman Emperor, Charles V. Charles was as fierce a Catholic as Edward was Protestant. If his cousin Mary was not allowed to hear mass, then he would invade England.

The pressure was off Mary for a time, but the Council continued to try to get at Mary through her servants. The Council disliked the fact that Mary's house was a haven for Catholics. (Many good Catholic families were desperate to have their daughters taken on as maids of honor, or even to go into Mary's service themselves. She had six chaplains, some of them distinguished academics.) When Mary came home late one day and one of her chaplains celebrated mass without her, an order went out for his arrest. At other times, members of her household, including Sir Robert Rochester, were summoned to court and ordered to influence Mary to change her ways.

No one in government was happy with the situation. And then, suddenly, as so often in Tudor politics, the situation changed abruptly. John Dudley started to be nice to Mary.

The explanation was not hard to find. Edward had become seriously ill with tuberculosis — the same illness that had killed his half brother, Henry Fitzroy. In February 1553, Mary was invited to court again. When she saw her brother she was shocked at how thin and feverish he looked. It was clear that he would not live long.

The question for Mary was this: Was Dudley being nice to her because he realized she would soon be Queen?

Elizabeth
My Sister Temperance
1549 – 1553

WHILE MARY WAS being treated as public enemy number one, Elizabeth steadily moved up in the court popularity stakes. But when John Dudley turned on the charm to Mary, he started to cold-shoulder Elizabeth.

It was true that Elizabeth had gotten off to a bad start. Her flirtation with Thomas Seymour while Queen Catherine was still alive had become public knowledge, and there were other rumors that made her sound even worse — for example, that Seymour had made her pregnant and that her illness the previous summer had been because of the loss of a baby. In other words, Elizabeth's reputation was in shreds in an age when reputation mattered a great deal.

Elizabeth spent the rest of 1549 doing the only thing she could to repair her reputation. She became a model of virtue, devoting herself to her studies, playing the lute and the virginals, and steering clear of unsuitable boyfriends.

When Somerset fell from power toward the end of 1549, it was great news for Elizabeth. She wrote to her brother, asking if she could come to court for Christmas. Edward said yes. Mary didn't join them that year. This was just as well, because Edward and the Council chose Christmas Day to inform all the bishops that they were not going to backtrack on the new prayer book. The Protestant reforms were going ahead.

Elizabeth was now 16, tall and slim, with long red hair that she wore loose down her back. At this time, she never wore bright colors or jewelry. Instead, she dressed plainly, often in black and white, the colors of a devout Protestant maiden. Edward was delighted with her. He liked the fact that his sister was so studious and quiet, that she wore plain clothes and didn't join in the dancing and flirtation at court. He called her "my sweet sister, Temperance." (Temperance means restraint.) What nobody could decide, then or since, was whether Elizabeth really was going through a devout phase or whether it was all an act.

The new imperial ambassador, Jehan Sheyfve, had no such doubts. He was convinced it was an act. He thought that Elizabeth was still the flirt she had always been and noted that her new target was John Dudley, the most powerful man in the land. Sheyfve spread the rumor that Dudley was planning to set his wife aside and marry Elizabeth, because the two spent so much time together and seemed to get along so well.

Sheyfve also noted the contrast in welcomes given to the two Tudor sisters in 1550, the year when both arrived for Christmas. Elizabeth was welcomed in splendid royal fashion, while Mary was practically ignored. He wrote:

They acted like this to show the people how much glory belongs to her who has embraced the new religion.

This was the year that Mary went home early. Elizabeth stayed for the big royal occasion of the year, Twelfth Night. Elizabeth played the role of king's consort at the huge banquet that year, eating at the same table as her brother and the French ambassador. Afterward, she and Edward went to watch bearbaiting with some of their courtiers.

Elizabeth was at the center of another huge procession the following year. In March 1552, she came to London with Dudley (now Duke of Northumberland) and Henry Grey, the Duke of Suffolk, in her train. The king had lent her St. James's Palace for her stay, a sign of great favor. Although she was second in line to the throne, to most people it must have looked as though she was the favorite.

But then, for some reason, the situation began to change. At first, people thought it might be because she had fallen out with the Duke of Northumberland over a palace. Before the Reformation, Durham Palace had been the Bishop of Durham's London residence. Elizabeth had inherited it from her father, but Northumberland wanted it for himself. So, without consulting Elizabeth, he had arranged for the palace to be given to him. In return he offered her Somerset House, which stands on the banks of the Thames. Elizabeth knew better than to make a fuss, but she was annoyed.

In February 1553, Elizabeth had also heard rumors that her brother was ill. Like Mary, she wanted to go to see him. But while Mary was allowed to see her brother, Elizabeth was stopped and turned back. She wrote her brother an agonized letter asking why. Was he displeased with her? What was going on? All she had to go on were rumors that he was very ill.

Elizabeth had grown up surrounded by people who thought it would be better for the country — and themselves — if she became queen after Edward. Some of those people were among Edward's advisers. Yet, at the crucial moment when Edward was dying, it was Elizabeth, not Mary, who was barred from his presence. She may not have understood exactly what it meant, but she must have guessed that it was not good news for her.

When Edward became ill, Mary and Elizabeth truly became rivals for the crown. Mary was the focus of hope for all those who longed for a return to Catholicism. Elizabeth was the one reformists wanted to see on the throne. But of course, nobody wanted either of them much, because nobody really wanted a queen, least of all Edward himself. Edward was a serious boy who had become increasingly extreme in his religious views and shared the strong dislike of women rulers shown by many Protestants. Five years later in Scotland, John Knox, the Protestant preacher, would write a pamphlet aimed at Mary Queen of Scots, cousin to Mary, Elizabeth, and Edward. He called it *The First Blast of the Trumpet Against the Monstrous Regiment of Women*, which gives us some idea of attitudes at the time.

Faced with the fact that he would not live long enough to father a child, Edward began poring over the history books in his sickroom. From what he read, it was quite obvious that in the past the crown had often been inherited from a mother. Edward decided this was all right, provided it was inherited by a son. What was quite wrong, thought Edward, was for a woman to rule in her own right.

Next, he looked to see who Henry had said should come next, if all his children died without heirs. It was Henry's youngest sister, Mary, and her descendants. Edward took this to mean her male descendants. He wrote his conclusions out by hand from his sickbed and called it *My Device for the Succession*.

The trouble with Edward's theory was that there were no male descendants there or anywhere else in the Tudor family. Mary and Elizabeth's Aunt Mary had no sons, and her three grandchildren were all female. These were the children of her daughter, Frances Brandon, who had married Henry Grey, Duke of Suffolk (an ally of Northumberland's who had ridden beside him in

Elizabeth's grandest procession). Grey's eldest daughter was Lady Jane Grey.

Jane was almost exactly the same age as Edward, and they had played together as children. Jane was a very scholarly girl and a strong Protestant. Elizabeth knew her well because Thomas Seymour had invited Jane to live at Chelsea Palace and share Elizabeth's lessons with Roger Ascham and other distinguished tutors.

Thomas Seymour had not taken Jane under his roof out of the goodness of his heart. He knew that she and Edward were very fond of each other and he persuaded her parents, who were very ambitious, that he could organize a marriage between their daughter and the young king. In fact, he had no power to choose Edward's wife for him, but the Grey parents believed that their daughter would one day be queen of England.

If Edward had lived, he and Jane might well have married. He may even have been in love with her, for many historians believe that, sick though he was, Edward played the driving role in what was happening behind the scenes. He was not put off by the lack of male heirs. Doubtless Jane would marry in time and produce a brood of children. Edward decreed that Jane Grey's "heirs male" were next in line to the throne.

Now Northumberland and Suffolk swung into action. It was important for Jane to be married and have a son as soon as possible. Jane's mother, Frances, told her that she was going to marry Northumberland's son, Guilford Dudley. Jane was horrified. She didn't like Guilford, and she didn't want to marry anyone. Her mother told her that she would do as she was told. When Jane continued to refuse she was beaten until she agreed.

The young couple were married with great splendor at Durham Palace on May 21, 1553. The celebrations went on for four days, and on the final day Jane's younger sister and Northumberland's daughter, both named Catherine, were also married to cement relationships among the Council and their allies.

A few days after the marriages, the king took a turn for the worse. Edward had been coughing up blood, but now, perhaps because of the treatment he was receiving from an old woman brought into the palace by Northumberland, Edward was sicker than ever. His hair and nails were falling out, and he had gangrene in his hands and feet. The old woman was a quack who had started feeding him arsenic. It was killing him faster than the disease.

There was now no chance that he would survive until Jane produced a baby, and Edward knew it. He asked for his document, *My Device for the Succession,* and changed the wording. His crown was now to go to Jane Grey *and* to her sons.

This obviously made complete nonsense of his theory about women. It was just arguable, in the tough world of English politics, that it was necessary to have a male ruler who could lead his troops into battle. But if there was no male ruler, then it was asking for trouble to push one woman out of the way for another.

In any case, not even the king of England could change the succession just like that. Edward needed the consent of Parliament, which was not sitting at the time. And it was doubtful whether Edward would live until Parliament could be recalled. Despite the terrible state of his health, Edward was determined. He summoned the Lord Chief Justice and law officers to his sickroom and ordered them to agree to his revised document. After consulting among themselves for some time, the judges came back and said that a king's decree couldn't overrule an Act of Succession passed by Parliament. Edward lost his temper and shouted at them, eyes glittering with fever in his wasted face. He reminded them that as justices they had sworn an oath of allegiance to the king.

The justices caved in. They agreed to put Edward's statement in proper legal form and added their own justification, which was that Henry's daughters were only of the "half-blood" — in other words, illegitimate. On June 21, the councillors signed the document. Those who were not part of the Northumberland-Suffolk alliance did so with grave misgivings. Three weeks later, Edward lay on his deathbed, and Northumberland sent messages to both Mary and Elizabeth. It was time to say a final farewell to their brother.

Mary

A Bloodless Revolution

1553

EVEN AS POOR EDWARD was drawing his last breath, a troop of soldiers, led by one of the toughest of Northumberland's camp, arrived at Hunsdon to arrest Mary and bring her to London. The kid gloves with which he had treated her in February were off. Now he was about to show her the iron fist.

In fact, Mary had set off for London before Northumberland's men arrived, intending to say her last good-bye to Edward as the Council requested. Remarkably, given the flurry of weddings among the most important reformist families, she does not seem to have realized what was going on. On the way to London, someone warned her that Northumberland was planning a coup. She then fled, disguised as a serving maid, to Kenninghall, in the middle of her own estates, where it would be harder to capture her.

At this point, Mary's chances of winning back her crown looked hopeless. Most of the noblemen in the country were either part of the conspiracy with Northumberland or afraid to speak out against it. As usual, Mary hoped the Holy Roman Emperor would come to her aid. She sent messages to his ambassadors. They were no help at all. Back came a message telling her to accept the situation and to make the best peace she could with Northumberland.

For once, Mary ignored their advice. This was her only chance to fulfill what she saw as her life's mission. The crown of England and the power it would give her to restore the Catholic faith — these were the reasons she had gone against her conscience and given in to her father all those years before. And so, against all the odds, Mary decided to go for it. On July 9, 1553, she ordered every member of her household to the great hall at Kenninghall, and there, a small, thin, rather worn woman of 38, she stood in the great chamber and in her deep voice announced that she was queen of England in both divine and human law. Her servants went wild, cheering and clapping. It was gratifying, but Mary knew that this was the easy part.

Jane was proclaimed queen in London on July 10. The very same day, Mary composed a letter to Northumberland and his fellow plotters. She scolded them soundly because she, the heir to the throne, had received no official notification of her brother's death. She told them that the succession had been laid down by Act of Parliament.

And she said she knew of the alternative arrangements they had made:

> But be it that some consideration politic hath hastily moved you thereto, yet doubt you not, my lords, we take all these your doings in gracious part, being also right ready to remit and fully pardon the same freely, to eschew bloodshed and vengeance.

In other words, she offered them an olive branch: If they changed course and supported her, she would pardon them. Mary then went on to say that she hoped she would not have to use force against them. Finally, she ordered them to proclaim her queen in London. The letter was sent to Northumberland, with copies to every city and town in the land. The effect was instantaneous, because away from London and outside the clique at court, most people saw right through Northumberland and thought what he was doing was an outrage.

Within days, minor gentry with their retainers, or followers, started flocking to Mary. Soon thousands had gathered at Kenninghall. At first, there was no one to organize them except for Mary's own household officers. But men kept coming, and with them news of a separate uprising in the Thames Valley. Soon the troops had to be moved to the larger, better fortified castle at Framlingham.

As news of this gathering army reached London,

Northumberland and his allies were worried. They knew they were unpopular. There had been a mutinous silence in the streets following proclamation of Jane as queen. The people had "murmured sore" when, the following Sunday, Bishop Ridley of London said from the pulpit that Mary and Elizabeth were both illegitimate. The law officers were doing what they could — a barman had had his ears cut off for shouting "Long live Queen Mary!" — but the resistance continued. And so did the stream of volunteers to fight for Mary.

It was clear that the rebellion had to be put down quickly and that Northumberland was the best man to do it. But Northumberland was needed in London to hold the Council together, so it was decided that Jane's father, the Duke of Suffolk, would go. For a reluctant queen, Jane was proving quite decisive. She had refused to make her husband, Guilford, king (much to Northumberland's disgust — the whole point of all this had been to bring the crown of England into his own family). And now she refused to let her father go and fight.

Northumberland had no choice but to go. He rode out of London, dressed in scarlet, at the head of an army. Just as he feared, his fellow plotters began to voice their secret doubts the moment his back was turned. The treasurer of the London Mint ran off to join Mary with all the gold in Queen Jane's exchequer (royal funds), and soldiers from Northumberland's conquering army began to desert in droves.

Mary, on the other hand, was riding high. Even

Protestant gentry were siding with her. There were now so many men under Mary's banner that her commander had lost count. When Mary rode by to inspect her troops her horse reared up, frightened by the noise from their guns. Mary dismounted and continued the inspection on foot. She had to walk more than a mile until she reached the end of the men.

Meanwhile, Jane tried to hold things together in London, but men were changing sides every day. Members of the Council defected until there were only three left. Finally, Northumberland was so desperate that he sent his cousin to France, laden with gold and jewelry, to try to enlist the French to his side.

Huge crowds had gathered to hear the Lord Mayor proclaim Mary queen in London on July 19. The mayor had to fight his way through them to the stone cross where the proclamation was traditionally made. In the Tower, Jane, still queen in name, heard bells pealing and the cheering of the people.

By evening, everyone had deserted Queen Jane except her closest personal servants. It was then that her father arrived, tore down the royal canopy over her throne, and told her brusquely that she was no longer queen. Then he disappeared as quickly as he had come, claiming he had always wanted Mary for queen. Jane was left to her fate.

Two days later, in a pathetic attempt to save his skin, Northumberland proclaimed Mary queen in Cambridge. He threw a hat full of gold coins in the air to show his enthusiasm. No one was impressed. On July 25, he was brought back to the capital under armed guard. Mary had become queen without so much as a single battle. She had triumphed over her Protestant cousin.

But what of her Protestant sister?

Elizabeth
Keeping Her Head
1553

THE MONTH THAT her brother died was every bit as dangerous for Elizabeth. Like Mary, she had received a summons from Northumberland to come to court at Greenwich to visit her brother. Northumberland was eager to have her where he could keep an eye on her. He knew that his plan would have many opponents and that the Protestants among them might gather around Elizabeth.

She received the summons on July 4, when Edward was just days from death. She must have suspected something was amiss, for she did not budge from Hatfield. She took to her bed and got a doctor to write a letter saying she was too sick to travel. Perhaps she was already more fully informed than people realized.

Edward died on July 6, though his death was kept secret for several days. Then, on July 10, came the news: Jane Grey had been declared queen and the authority for this lay in Edward's *My Device for the Succession*. Elizabeth must have been in turmoil.

The order of succession, which her powerful father had laid down and to which Parliament had agreed, had been tossed aside in favor of a last-minute change thought up by a dying boy. And all the most powerful men in the country were lined up behind the new arrangement.

It was an enormous slap in the face to Elizabeth and explained why Northumberland had not wanted her to see Edward back in February. She and Edward had been close as children, and if Edward wanted a Protestant heir to the throne, then Elizabeth was the obvious choice. Elizabeth herself must have dreaded Mary becoming queen of England, but she believed strongly in the monarchy. She knew that less than a century before the country had been plunged into a civil war that lasted more than 30 years because of a dispute over the succession. The wars had caused misery and loss of life, and they had come to an end only when her strong grandfather, Henry VII, seized power. One of Elizabeth's virtues when she became queen was that she would not send men to fight if she could possibly avoid it.

Elizabeth knew that her own claim to the throne derived from her father's authority. She probably agreed with the order that he had laid down, which was the same as if all three children were legitimate. So she had decided to play by her father's rules. Yet in playing by those rules, she had been swept aside, along with Mary.

(If the coup had succeeded and the people had accepted Jane as queen, then the crown would have gone next to her heirs. Elizabeth would have lost out on the succession entirely.)

The question of how to respond was urgent. If she acknowledged Jane as queen, then not only was she giving up her own birthright, she was committing treason against Mary, the rightful queen. If she protested, then Northumberland could accuse her of treason against his daughter-in-law, Queen Jane. Whichever side she chose, there was the possibility of having to face the executioner as her mother had done. No wonder Elizabeth kept to her bed and waited to see what would happen next.

It is hard to imagine what it must have been like, waiting for news in a world with no phones, radio, or television. Elizabeth would have depended on messengers on horseback. The news might be out of date by the time a messenger arrived. But the news did arrive — first that Mary had declared herself queen, then that the people were flocking to fight for her, and finally that Northumberland was in the Tower awaiting trial. There was other news, too: On two of the three Sundays that Jane was queen, the Bishop of London had preached from the pulpit that Mary and Elizabeth were "not lawfully begotten in the estate of true matrimony according to God's law." Elizabeth stored this information quietly for future use. She was certainly finding out who her friends were.

Once it was clear that Mary had won out over Northumberland and the rebels, Elizabeth wrote her a letter of congratulation. She asked her sister whether she would wear mourning for Edward when they met, which suggests that she felt Mary would be quite within her rights if she decided not to mourn him — and also that Elizabeth wanted to make it quite clear that she would follow Mary's lead.

Mary told Elizabeth to meet her in London. Miraculously better from her mystery illness, Elizabeth rode out from Hatfield, surrounded by her own supporters. There were two thousand of them, the men among them armed with spears, bows, and guns. This huge procession — half army, half ceremonial escort — rode through the narrow streets of London, taking the queen's half sister — now heir to the throne — to Somerset House. Was Elizabeth trying to tell Mary something? Her people wore green and white, the Tudor colors, which emphasized her descent, her blood, and her birthright. And their number was proof that, unlike Jane, she was a power to be reckoned with.

Mary no doubt heard of Elizabeth's triumphant arrival in London. Theirs was a difficult relationship, and they had not seen each other for more than two years. During most of this time Elizabeth had been the favored sister, embracing the new religion and being treated with the honor that was denied to Mary. Now the tables were turned, and Mary was the one with the power to bestow or withhold favor. Elizabeth rode out to Wanstead the following day, with a tactfully smaller escort, to greet her queen. When she saw Mary at the head of a large procession, advancing toward her, she knelt in homage on the muddy Colchester road. Mary appeared pleased to see her. She raised Elizabeth up and kissed her. A couple of days later, they made a ceremonial entry, together, into London. Mary was dressed in deepest purple, the color of royalty, embroidered with gold and gems. Elizabeth still wore black and white, with few adornments.

The crowd cheered them both: their 38-year-old queen, and her tall, striking, 19-year-old half sister. For the people in the streets that day, their presence side by side was a symbol of hope. They could all, Catholic and Protestant, put their religious differences aside and live peacefully according to the order of succession that King Henry VIII had laid down.

For the moment, the question of who would succeed to the throne had been answered. Mary had done so. The sisters were rivals no more. Or were they?

Queen of England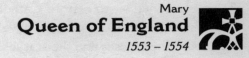
1553 – 1554

MARY'S FIRST TASK as queen was to deal with the rebels. She had promised to be merciful, but Simon Reynard, the imperial ambassador, thought differently. He advised Mary to execute Jane and her husband and anyone else who threatened her authority. Mary refused. She thought Jane was a self-righteous girl — there had been an incident when Jane, staying with Mary, had mocked one of Mary's servants for curtseying to the bread used in Holy Communion. However, Mary was sure that Jane and Guilford had been mere puppets, and that Northumberland, Suffolk, and their allies were the real culprits in the plot to deprive her of her throne. So although Guilford and Jane were found guilty of treason, they were not executed. They were kept in the Tower, with the unspoken understanding that in time they would be pardoned. Guilford's father, Northumberland, and two others were executed. All three of them renounced their Protestant faith and took Catholic Communion before they died.

Next Mary turned to the task for which she believed she was destined — to restore Catholicism to England. The first thing she did was to have the old religious symbols — the crosses and the statues — put back in the royal chapels. At this stage, Mary was not forcing her subjects to worship according to Catholic rites, but the pressure to do so at court was intense. Mass was said several times at day, and everyone at court was expected to attend, including Elizabeth.

Also, at last, Mary was free to marry. Of course, she was hoping for love and companionship, but she also felt that as a woman she needed a husband to help her rule the kingdom. Most important of all, she hoped that she might still bear a child — a male, Catholic heir to the throne, which would put Elizabeth out of the running once and for all.

Her subjects agreed with her that a woman could not rule on her own. They wanted her to marry an Englishman: Edward Courtenay, last seen disappearing into the Tower when that fateful coat of arms had been found in Margaret Pole's house in 1539. Edward and his mother had languished in the Tower all that time until 1553, when Mary released them. He was now a young man, with his own claim to the throne — his father had been a cousin of Henry VIII's.

Mary, however, was not the least bit interested in Edward Courtenay. She had her eye on Europe. She was, after all, half Spanish, and throughout her troubled life, when everyone else had rejected her, her rights, and her beliefs, she had found friends in the imperial ambassadors of the Holy Roman Empire, who represented Charles V, the very man to whom Mary had been engaged when she was six and he was 22.

Charles was now 54 and a widower. He wanted an alliance with England, not least because his old enemy, the king of France, had promised his eldest son to the infant Mary Queen of Scots. (The old quarrel between France and the Holy Roman Empire was as strong as ever.) In addition, Charles was a militant Catholic who had spent many years persecuting the Protestants in Flanders and Germany. To bring a Catholic England into the fold of the Holy Roman Empire would be a triumph. It would also mean that there was nowhere for his Protestant rebels to hide and regroup.

However, Charles did not plan to marry Mary. Instead, he offered his son: Philip, Prince of Spain, blond, good-looking, 26 years old, and a bit of a ladies' man. In the October following her coronation Mary knelt with the imperial ambassador and one of her closest waiting women and prayed for guidance on the marriage. Then Mary rose and announced that "Philip was the chosen of Heaven for her, the Virgin Queen."

How could her Council argue with that? By November, she had steamrollered them into agreement. Later that month, the House of Commons sent their speaker to beg her to think again. In their view, it would better for her "to marry within the Realm." In other words, they still wanted

Mary to marry an Englishman. Mary was furious. She replied that Parliament had no right to tell her what to do:

> We* have heard much from you of the incommodities which may attend our marriage; we have not heard from you of the commodities thereof, one of which is of some weight with us, namely, of our private inclination. We have not forgotten our coronation oath. We shall marry as God shall direct our choice, to his honour and our country's good.

In January 1554, a delegation of Spaniards arrived to negotiate the terms of the marriage. They were pelted with snowballs by boys in the streets, and there was no cheering as they passed. The fear among Englishmen and women was that England would become nothing but a satellite of the great Holy Roman Empire, ruled not by its English sovereign but by Spain and the Empire.

Soon it wasn't just snowballs and silence in the streets. That same month, a rebellion was underway, led by Sir Thomas Wyatt and Lady Jane Grey's father, Henry (who had escaped execution for putting his daughter on the throne), together with Sir Peter Carew in the southwest and Sir James Croft on the Welsh border. Their plan was to march on London and prevent the Spanish marriage. French warships were standing by in the Channel to send men ashore if needed. According to the French ambassador, the rebels also planned to

* It is traditional for a monarch to use the word "we" to mean himself or herself in their royal role.

dethrone Mary and replace her with Elizabeth. Elizabeth would then be married to Edward Courtenay.

No one seems to have consulted Courtenay about this. He was angry that Mary had passed him over for Philip of Spain, but he did not want to marry Elizabeth and he told on the plotters. As a result, most of the uprisings failed even to get started. Only Wyatt went ahead with his plans.

Mary ordered the 80-year-old Duke of Norfolk to go to Kent and put down the rebels (20 years earlier he had been sent to tell Mary she was no longer a princess). Half his soldiers defected to Wyatt, and the other half fled back to London with their coats turned inside out so that no one should see the royal coat of arms. Now Wyatt was marching on London. The question was, would Londoners flock to his standard as he hoped? If so, Elizabeth might soon be queen.

Just as she had done when Northumberland had proclaimed Jane as queen, Mary now rose to the occasion. She gave a rousing speech to the burghers, or wealthy citizens, of London, which swung them over to her side. In the chaos of the next day, when a contingent of Wyatt's men almost overran Whitehall Palace, her servants were crying with fear, and the imperial envoys wanted to make a run for it, Mary kept her head again. The palace gates were barred, Wyatt was defeated, and by nightfall on February 7, 1554, he was a prisoner in the Tower of London.

Mary was safe, but Elizabeth was on the brink of the most dangerous period of her life.

"Much Suspected of Me"

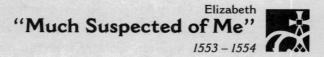

ELIZABETH HAD BEEN having a tough time ever since her brother fell ill. First, there had been Northumberland's refusal to let her see Edward. Then had come her brother's death and the discovery that she had been betrayed by the very people she thought were her political allies (including her cousins Jane Grey and her sisters). Whereas for Mary 1553 had ended well, for Elizabeth things were getting worse. The encouraging moment when she had ridden at Mary's side as she entered London had been just that — a moment. From then on, there was constant pressure on her to attend mass, and ultimately to become a Catholic. For Mary that would have been a tremendous coup — all but the most committed Protestants would follow Elizabeth's lead and turn Catholic.

Elizabeth knew that this was not the only reason Mary wanted her to attend mass. Mary genuinely believed that hers was the one true Church. The unspoken threat was that if Elizabeth did not do as Mary said, Mary would have to think again about Elizabeth as her heir.

Mary had been put in a similar position by her father, and she had been prepared to die for her faith. But not Elizabeth. She had no intention of becoming a martyr. She would do whatever it took to survive. And so when Mary started getting at her about not going to mass, Elizabeth played for time and asked her if she could be instructed in the Catholic religion so that she could make an informed decision. When Mary upped the pressure, she went to Catholic services, but with bad grace. She didn't want her Protestant supporters thinking she really had turned Catholic.

The trouble for both sisters was that their differences over religion weren't just about what they actually believed. There was all the other emotional baggage going right back to Mary's adolescence and Elizabeth's birth. For as well as negotiating with the pope to bring the Church of England back under the umbrella of Catholicism, Mary began her reign by asking Parliament to reverse all the religious changes of Edward's reign, plus Henry's Acts of Succession and Supremacy. What this meant in practice was that Mary's mother's marriage to Henry was declared valid, and her own birth legitimate. And the inevitable consequence of this was that Henry had had no right to marry Anne Boleyn, and that Elizabeth's illegitimate status was confirmed. From here it was one short, logical step to saying that

Elizabeth should not and could not be heir to the throne. As if to highlight this, Mary suddenly decided that Elizabeth should no longer have the place of honor beside her at court. Perhaps going over all the old arguments had brought back memories of the days when she had been forced to curtsy to Elizabeth and walk behind her in processions. Instead, Margaret, Countess of Lennox, a cousin of Mary and Elizabeth's and daughter of Henry VIII's eldest sister, took Elizabeth's place. Margaret Lennox was a Catholic. It was not surprising that, in Mary's eyes, she would make a much more suitable successor than Elizabeth.

By the end of November 1553, the Tudor sisters were barely on speaking terms. Elizabeth was so clearly out of favor that courtiers were afraid to be seen talking to her. She asked Mary's permission to go home for Christmas. Mary, who had been told by the imperial ambassador, Simon Renard, that Elizabeth was in secret communication with the French ambassador, Antoine de Noailles, was glad to see her leave. It is from these two ambassadors that we know of their parting. To the Frenchman, it looked as if the two sisters were back on friendly terms, especially when Mary gave Elizabeth a gift of a double rope of pearls and a sable hood. According to Renard, this was all a pretence. "I had much difficulty persuading her to dissemble [pretend]," he said.

Elizabeth left, begging Mary not to listen to false rumors about her and to give her the chance to speak for herself. Mary agreed and watched her go, escorted by five hundred horsemen. What Elizabeth may not have known was that Mary had planted two spies in Elizabeth's household. She did not trust her sister at all.

Ten miles from London, Elizabeth sent a messenger back to Mary, asking for chasubles, copes, and other objects used in Catholic worship. It seems strange that she did not think of this before she left. Could she perhaps have heard what had happened that day in London? That a dog, with its head shaved like a priest and with a hangman's noose around its neck, had been thrown into the queen's Presence Chamber, together with a note saying that all priests should be hanged? Was she trying to distance herself from this event?

In fact, the country was in uproar, not because Mary was at odds with Elizabeth but because of her marriage plans and the fear that England would be lost in the huge Holy Roman Empire.

Early in 1554, while she was living at her house at Ashridge, Elizabeth received a letter from Sir Thomas Wyatt. In it he told her that he was raising a rebellion in her name. Elizabeth did not reply, but neither did she inform Mary of Wyatt's letter. However, when his rebellion failed, it meant trouble for Elizabeth. Simon Reynard, the imperial ambassador, wrote to his master, Charles V, telling him that Mary meant to execute both Elizabeth and Edward Courtenay.

The first people to die for the Wyatt rebellion were Guilford Dudley and Jane Grey. They had been sentenced to death nine months earlier, but Mary had delayed their execution, and it was expected that after her marriage she would pardon them. Yet on February 12, four days after Wyatt was defeated, Mary avenged herself on the Duke of Suffolk, for taking part in a second rebellion. Guilford Dudley was beheaded on Tower Hill. Later that day it was Jane's turn. She was just 17.

The news, when it reached Elizabeth, must have been chilling. Neither Guilford nor Jane had had anything to do with the Wyatt rebellion. If this was what Mary did to people who weren't even involved, what might she do to Elizabeth? The Wyatt rebellion had been in her name.

Already Mary had sent three of her privy councillors to Ashridge with a troop of men to bring Elizabeth in, but by this time Elizabeth was genuinely and seriously ill, possibly from stress. She was in pain and her body had lumps as a result of what is thought to have been a kidney problem.

Ill or not, the councillors insisted that they start out for London. Elizabeth was so ill that she had to travel in a litter, and the group could only manage six miles a day. When they reached the outskirts of London, she insisted that the curtains of the litter be opened so that people could see her, dressed in white and very pale.

Elizabeth hoped to be able to speak to Mary and convince her of her loyalty, but when she finally reached Whitehall Palace, Mary refused to see her. She was given a room distant from the rest of the court, clearly in disgrace, but where Mary could keep a close eye on her.

Mary was certain Elizabeth had known of the planned uprisings. Now, as the plotters were interrogated, it emerged that Sir James Croft had visited Elizabeth at Ashridge on the way to his lands on the Welsh border. It also came out that Wyatt had advised Elizabeth to move to her safe, well-fortified house at Donnington. In addition, Mary's agents had found a copy of the letter that Elizabeth had sent to Mary in the possession of the French ambassador. It could have meant that either Elizabeth or someone close to her was plotting with the French. None of this was conclusive proof that she was involved with Wyatt, but added together, it looked very likely. If only Wyatt or one of the others could be made to reveal more.

Amazingly, given the cruelty of Tudor interrogations, nobody did. All that Wyatt would say was that he had written to Elizabeth and that she had sent a verbal reply. The message was, "she did thank him much for his good will, and she would do as she should see cause."

Nevertheless, Elizabeth was now charged with conspiring with Wyatt and the others. If found guilty, this was treason, and the sentence was death.

Within an hour, Elizabeth was under armed guard. The next day, two of Mary's councillors arrived to take her by barge to the Tower of London. The reason she was to travel by river was so that fewer people would see her pass. Mary was all too aware of Elizabeth's popularity.

At this point, Elizabeth was terrified. The Tower was the prison for state prisoners, and more often than not their last home before they were executed. She begged the councillors to be allowed to write to her sister before she left. At first they said no, but Elizabeth pleaded and pleaded, and finally, they allowed her to do as she wished.

The letter Elizabeth wrote that day still exists. In it she reminded Mary of the promise she had made before Christmas — that no matter what bad things she heard about Elizabeth, she would see Elizabeth and allow her to tell her version of what had happened. Then she told Mary what Thomas Seymour had said before he died — that if his brother had heard what he had to say, he would never have ordered his death.

Of the actual charges against her she said:

> And as for the traitor Wyatt, he might peradventure write me a letter, but on my faith I never received any from him. And as for the letter sent to the French king, I pray God confound me if I ever sent him word, message, token or letter.

Below her signature, she drew a row of lines diagonally across the remainder of the page so that no one could add anything. By the time she had finished, it was late. The tide was too low for the barge to reach the Tower safely that night. Mary was furious when she heard and scolded her councillors for letting Elizabeth run rings around them.

The following day she was taken to the Tower. It was a rainy Sunday morning, and there was no one around. Legend has it that she was taken through the gate right on the river, called Traitors' Gate, but it is more likely that she disembarked at Tower Wharf and walked in over the drawbridge.

It is easy now, knowing that Elizabeth survived, to think that her stay in the Tower was just a short, unpleasant episode. But for Elizabeth, at the time, not knowing the future, it must have seemed like the lead-up to her death. Her apartments were those in which her mother had lodged during the days before her execution. The scaffold on which Jane Grey had been beheaded still stood in one of the courtyards. Elizabeth was cut off from all support, allowed no visitors, and not allowed to write or receive letters.

The one crumb of comfort was that her jailers were arguing among themselves about how to treat her. Some were for locking the doors on her. Others thought that was unwise, for it had happened before that today's prisoner was tomorrow's king or queen.

Over the days that followed, Elizabeth was brought before the Council. They wanted to know all about Donnington. Why had she been planning to go there? Elizabeth tried to be vague — did she actually have a house at Donnington, she asked? Then she said she remembered that of course she did, but she had never stayed there. The Council summoned another of their prisoners, Sir James Croft, who apologized for naming her and explained that he had been roughly interrogated: "I have been marvellously tossed and examined touching Your Highness." Now Elizabeth said it came back to her — she remembered her servants talking with Sir James about Donnington, but that it had nothing do with her, and what did it matter anyway? Surely, she could go to any of her houses whenever she chose?

Elizabeth had probably guessed, when Mary sent a message to Ashridge and ordered her not to go to Donnington, that the government was aware of a buildup of arms and food supplies there. Elizabeth's only hope was to persuade the Council that she knew nothing about it.

Elizabeth was good at saying nothing, at barefaced denial. The problem was her servants. Would someone say something that left her exposed? On a window in the Tower, there is an inscription, supposedly carved with a diamond:

MUCH SUSPECTED OF ME
NOTHING PROVED CAN BE.

It is said to have been scratched by Elizabeth.

Wyatt had been offered a pardon if he would point the finger at Elizabeth. He refused and was executed the following month, on April 11.

Much to the government's annoyance, he made a speech from the scaffold. He said:

And whereas it is said and whistled abroad that I should accuse my Lady Elizabeth's grace and my Lord Courtenay, it is not so, good people. For I assure you neither they nor any other now in yonder hold or durance was privy of my rising or commotion before I began. As I have declared no less to the Queen's Council. And this is most true.

Wyatt was turning into a hero in the people's eyes. His head, stuck on a pike to deter others, was stolen by sympathizers. Then another of the conspirators was acquitted. A second jury had to be assembled to convict Sir James Croft, as only eight of the 12 jurors were prepared to find him guilty the first time around. With so much sympathy for the conspirators, the Council, already divided among themselves, realized it might be dangerous to try Elizabeth publicly.

Elizabeth did not know this, of course. At the beginning of May, she heard the sound of a troop of armed men marching into the Tower courtyard. She was convinced they had come to escort her to her execution and asked if Jane Grey's scaffold was still standing. It had been dismantled.

Then a new jailer appeared. He was Sir Henry Bedingfield, one of the knights who had joined Mary right at the beginning when she raised her standard at Kenninghall. He had come to take Elizabeth to new quarters.

Elizabeth panicked. So they were not going to put her on trial. Instead, she was going to disappear quietly and without a trace, like other inconvenient royal prisoners had in the past. "If my murdering was secretly committed to your charge, would you see to the execution thereof?" she is supposed to have asked him.

Bedingfield was offended. He told her he was there to protect her from attack by her enemies — and rescue by her friends. For across the city, away from the Tower, feelings were still running high about the queen's marriage and Wyatt's attempt to prevent it. Weeks after the leaders of the Wyatt rebellion had been executed, their followers were still being hanged and beheaded on gallows across London, their bodies left on display to warn off other rebels.

For the same reason as before, Elizabeth was spirited out of the city along the river. It was supposed to be a secret, but word had leaked out, and along the Thames people gathered, cheering and waving as they saw her barge and its escorts pass. After a night at Richmond Palace, Elizabeth was taken by road to Woodstock in Oxfordshire. A group of her own servants had heard that she was to pass that way and were waiting to give her an encouraging wave. Over the next four days, Eton schoolboys turned out to see her, and well-wishers lined her route. At one village, Bedingfield had the bell ringers arrested, while at High Wycombe women had baked cakes for her and loaded them into her litter. There were so many she had to ask them to stop. It was a strange progress for a prisoner of the queen, and it made Bedingfield nervous. As for Elizabeth, it must have given her hope. In disgrace with her sister she might be, but the people loved her, and their love would make it dangerous for Mary to kill her.

Over and over again, Elizabeth spoke of her fear that she would be secretly murdered. By voicing it, she was doing what she could to alert others to suspect any accident or mysterious illness that might befall her.

Woodstock near Oxford had been chosen as the place in which Elizabeth was to live under house arrest. It was a large, rambling, rather run-down palace. To Bedingfield's concern — and probably to Elizabeth's secret delight — there were only three doors in the entire place that could be locked. Better still, there was not room for all of her servants and Bedingfield's to live in the house, so Elizabeth's steward, Thomas Parry, took rooms at the Bull Inn. It made some sense, because in cases of house arrest like this it was up to the prisoner to pay for the food for the jailer and his staff, and it was easier for Parry to organize supplies for the house from the town. But it also made it easier for him to meet with messengers and hatch plots, and this is exactly what Parry did, shamelessly. And so Elizabeth was kept informed of what was happening in the country, and more or less anyone who wanted to pass a message to her could do so.

She was, however, still a prisoner. She could not leave the house nor receive visitors. And she found her jailer deeply irritating. Bedingfield was a man who performed his duty to the letter. He was completely loyal to Mary and immune to Elizabeth's charm. He interpreted all his instructions literally. This drove Elizabeth mad. It wasn't much fun for Bedingfield, either. He found himself defeated by everything: the ramshackle house, constantly in need of repair; the unsatisfactory security; and the cleverness of Elizabeth and her servants. Matters were made worse by the fact that he had to kneel to Elizabeth whenever he addressed her, and she was in charge of their joint finances.

At first, Bedingfield forbade Elizabeth to write to Mary. Then he received a letter from the Council with a postscript from the queen saying she would be pleased to hear from Elizabeth. Elizabeth wrote, protesting her ignorance of the Wyatt plot and all the preparations that accompanied it. Mary wrote to Bedingfield, saying that it was funny how Elizabeth's letters had been found in the French ambassador's bag and strange that the plotters had wanted to put Elizabeth on the throne. She told Elizabeth she wanted no more of her pretense and her "colourable letters." She was to set matters straight with God, and then maybe she would behave as she should toward her sovereign.

For Elizabeth, this was one of the most fraught issues. When Mary talked about Elizabeth's relationship with God, she was really talking about her progress with Catholicism. Elizabeth was doing what Mary asked and worshipping according to Catholic rites, except for one thing. She still read her English Bible, not the Latin one, and used certain English prayers. Mary heard of this from Bedingfield and sent a message that from now on

Elizabeth would use Latin prayers like everyone else. Elizabeth protested but in the end did as she was told.

The weeks at Woodstock turned into months. Both Bedingfield and Elizabeth had had enough of the drafty house. They were also sick and tired of each other. Meanwhile, news came to Elizabeth via Thomas Parry. Mary was married. Then, unbelievably, Mary was pregnant. It must have seemed to Elizabeth that everything in the garden was wonderful for Mary, while her own life had ground to a halt. No wonder she was difficult. Now when her chaplain prayed for "Thy servants Philip our King and Mary our Queen," Elizabeth stayed obstinately silent at the moment she was supposed to respond. Mary might still be her queen, but she did not consider Philip her king. Bedingfield reported this behavior to Mary.

Married at Last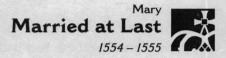

1554 – 1555

THE WYATT REBELLION of 1554 had shown Mary that winning her crown was not enough. She had to hold on to it. And she worried that the unrest in the country would make Philip not want to marry her. Already he seemed less eager for the marriage than she would have wished. Although English and Spanish envoys were passing messages to and from her future husband, he had not bothered to write to her directly. This lapse was causing tongues to wag. Didn't Philip want to marry her? "She is nothing but a poor, love-sick woman," reported the French ambassador, Antoine de Noailles, early in 1554.

Finally, there was relief for Mary on that score. On May 11, 1554, she received her first letter. It had been written and sent months before. With it, Philip sent her two diamond necklaces and another priceless jewel that had belonged to her grandmother Isabella of Castile.

Mary was moved. At last, she was marrying into the safety and protection of her mother's family. Perhaps it was no coincidence that nine days later, Elizabeth was removed from the Tower and sent on her trip to Woodstock. Mary may have felt safer, knowing that things were going according to plan. The marriage really was going ahead, and with it the possibility of an heir, which would ensure that everything that Mary was doing to bring England back to Catholicism was undisturbed.

In June, the fleet carrying Philip's advance party was sighted from the Isle of Wight. One hundred and twenty-five Spanish sailing ships, carrying nine thousand noblemen, soldiers, and servants, a thousand horses and mules, and three million gold ducats, were heading for the English coast. Charles V had told his son that he should arrive with the "minimum of display," so his nine thousand retainers would not all come ashore. Once in England, he would have only his personal guard. It was up to Mary to guarantee his safety. But Philip was not even aboard any of the ships. He was away fighting a war, although it was said he would arrive within two weeks.

Philip arrived in July. Mary set off for Winchester, laden with presents for him. She had sent him the gift of a beautiful white horse with red velvet trappings bound with gold. Philip tried to be polite to his new subjects-to-be, drinking beer like the English and joking that his clothes — which were super rich and fashionable — were not good enough to marry the English queen. After three rain-soaked days in Southampton, he rode to Winchester to meet Mary. The rain was lashing down, the road was muddy, and by the time he reached Winchester, his white satin outfit was ruined. Philip changed into clothes of black velvet.

That evening, after attending mass in Winchester Cathedral, Philip and Mary met face-to-face for the first time. She was overwhelmed at her luck. He was blond, young, and handsome. Philip was less impressed with Mary. There was no way he would ever have married her if it were not for affairs of state. His courtiers felt sorry for him. Ruy Gomez, one of his closest advisers, said that Mary was older than they had been told: "She is not at all beautiful and flabby rather than fat. She is of white complexion and fair, and has no eyebrows." Another Spaniard remarked unchivalrously that she had lost most of her teeth.

Philip and Mary were married in Winchester Cathedral on July 25. His father had made him king of Naples for the occasion so that he was of equal royal status with Mary. He wore a white doublet and breeches and a gold cloak lined with crimson satin. Mary wore a black velvet dress and a cloak that matched Philip's. There were so many jewels stitched to the dress and around her throat that "the eye was blinded to look upon her." She was attended by 50 gentlewomen dressed in cloth of gold and silver. Because of what had happened in Henry and

Edward's reigns, England was still excommunicated (expelled) from the Catholic Church and so not allowed to take part in Catholic services. This meant that Mary had to ask the pope for a dispensation, or official letter, saying that her marriage was lawful. After the two-hour ceremony, followed by Communion mass, the couple were declared:

> Philip and Mary, by the grace of God, King and Queen of England, France, Naples, Jerusalem and Ireland, defenders of the faith, Princes of Spain and Sicily, Archdukes of Austria, Dukes of Milan, Burgundy and Brabant, Counts of Hapsburg, Flanders and the Tyrol.

Next day, Philip's courtiers appeared at Mary's door, according to the Spanish custom, demanding to be allowed in to see the happy couple. Mary's ladies-in-waiting were shocked. This was not the way things were done in England. In any case, Philip was not there. He had been up since the crack of dawn, working on state papers.

There were many other tensions. Even at the wedding feast, the Spanish were offended because Mary ate from gold plates, while Philip ate from silver. And in the following weeks there were numerous scuffles between Englishmen and Spaniards. By the end of September, there were fights at court nearly every day. The French ambassador thought (and probably hoped) that there was a plot afoot for the English to murder all the Spaniards, including Philip and the queen.

Meanwhile, Mary thought herself the luckiest of women. She had married into Europe and into her mother's family, *and* she was head over heels in love with her husband. Now she had only two ambitions left: to bear a son and to return England to the Catholic Church.

The following September, Mary's doctors gave her the best news in the world — she was pregnant. This calmed the warring hooligans of the court and the streets. And it made Mary all the more determined that England should finally rejoin the mainstream of Catholic Christianity. That same September, she ordered her Council to send for the pope's ambassador to England, Reginald Pole. (This was the man who had fallen afoul of Henry VIII; his mother, Mary's godmother, had hoped he and Mary might marry. He had been living in Rome but had moved to Flanders, knowing this summons was about to come.) Pole's job would be to supervise an inspection of what was being taught in English universities and preached in the churches. Any Protestants (or heretics as Mary thought of them) were to be burned at the stake.

Pole arrived back in England in November 1554. It was the first time Mary had seen him for more than 20 years. As he stepped forward to greet her, she thought she felt a movement in her womb. It was probably excitement, but Mary took it as a sign from God that she was on the right track. So did Pole. He greeted her with the words from the Bible that the angel said to Jesus's mother when he told her she was pregnant, "Blessed art thou among women and blessed is the fruit of thy womb."

Over the next few months, the country continued its journey back into the arms of the Catholic Church. Parliament was led by Gardiner, Bishop of Winchester, in an apology on behalf of the whole country for "the disobedience committed in this Realm" against the pope and the Church of Rome. In return, Pole granted forgiveness to the whole kingdom on the pope's behalf and said that, each year, the day should be celebrated as the Feast of Reconciliation.

This had all been achieved with Philip's help. He had worked behind the scenes with various members of the queen's Council. But Philip wasn't having an easy ride. His father expected him to rule England in Mary's name, but Mary wasn't always willing to take Philip's advice. In her view, she was queen and he was only her consort. This bothered Philip, and — on top of the fact that he did not find his wife very attractive — was another reason he felt restless in his marriage.

One of the subjects over which Philip and Mary disagreed was the policy of burning heretics. Although Philip was enthusiastic about the Inquisition, which tortured and burned heretics back home in Spain, he did not want his English subjects to think that it was he who was bringing the policy to England. For the sake of his own standing, he told Mary to go carefully. But that was the last thing Mary wanted to do. It was as if she were making up for all the years she had felt powerless at the hands of Protestants. She was determined to get rid of every heretic in the country.

By December 1554, Parliament had passed an act that allowed the bishops to investigate people suspected of heresy. Those they found guilty would be handed over to the government for burning. Their property would be given to the crown. Unsurprisingly, as this act came into force, lots of Protestants decided to go into exile abroad.

Meanwhile, all the time that Elizabeth was a prisoner, Mary received reports of her sister. She would have known of the impudence with which Elizabeth and her servants treated Henry Bedingfield. She would have heard about the comings and goings around the Bull Inn. The news that Elizabeth would not pray for Mary's husband, the king, just proved what Mary knew all along: that Elizabeth was as rebellious as ever.

What probably saved Elizabeth was the other, galling news that had come to Mary — that on Elizabeth's trip to Woodstock, she had been welcomed and cheered by thousands of people. Mary knew that Elizabeth was popular for all sorts of reasons — her Protestantism, her youth, and her beauty. Above all, she was popular because, in the eyes of the people, she was an all-English princess. Mary knew that she would have to have rock-solid proof of Elizabeth's treason before she could execute her. Refusal to include Philip's name in her prayers was not enough. Too many of Mary's subjects felt the same way.

There may have been many unhappy people in the country, but the end of 1554 saw Mary at her happiest. Christmas at court was celebrated in splendid style. Then, in January 1555, came the first of the burnings. First to die was a married clergyman named John Rogers, of St. Paul's Cathedral in London. Crowds gathered to watch him go to his death. They were not cheering for Mary. They were angry because Rogers had been refused permission to say good-bye to his wife and children.

Mary was unperturbed by this. She was certain that she was right. She was doing the heretics a favor, for Rogers's agony was just a foretaste of the pain of the fires of hell, which Mary believed awaited every heretic. Perhaps by watching Rogers, others might give up their "wrong" opinions, return to the Catholic Church, and be spared the fires of hell.

Much more troubling to Mary than the pain of a few heretics was the fact that Philip wanted to go back to Europe. The war between France and the Empire rumbled on, and he wrote to his father to tell him that he wanted to lead a campaign. His father advised him to stay until the baby was born. Philip, who was bored and fed up, amused himself by taking part in tournaments at court. Mary refused to watch, so frightened was she that her beloved husband would hurt himself.

In April, the royal pair moved to Hampton Court, where it was planned that Mary would have her baby. An immense amount of planning had been done. Doctors, midwives, wet nurses, and women to rock the cradle were lined up. In the royal bedroom stood a huge ornate wooden cradle, carved with a prayer:

> The child which Thou to Mary,
> O Lord of Might, hast send
> To England's joy, in health preserve,
> keep and defend.

Mary and her ladies had embroidered a quilt for this cradle and for Mary's bed. The great day of Mary's final triumph was approaching, for if the child lived, England would have a Catholic heir, and Elizabeth's chance of succession would be all but over.

Was this why Mary ordered Sir Henry Bedingfield to bring Elizabeth to Hampton Court? Was it that she wanted Elizabeth to witness her triumph? Or was it because Mary knew that things could still go terribly wrong? Her own mother had had a series of miscarriages and stillbirths. For the sixteenth century, Mary was unusually old to be having her first baby. She might not survive the birth. Did she — or Philip — want Elizabeth where they could keep an eye on her should things go wrong?

Elizabeth

The Injured Innocent
1555

FOR ELIZABETH, IT WAS both a huge relief and a scary moment when the summons came for her to go to Hampton Court. On the one hand, it could mean that the terrible tedium of her imprisonment was about to end. On the other, that she would have to face Mary, and somehow convince her that she had never plotted against her. Although Elizabeth had found it fun to annoy Bedingfield, she must always have been aware that behind Bedingfield stood Mary. By this time, Mary had shown everyone how cruel she could be — to both political and religious rebels.

On April 20, 1555, Elizabeth set off from Woodstock, escorted by Sir Henry and a troop of men. It wasn't a good day to travel. It was blowing a gale, and so Elizabeth sensibly suggested that they seek shelter until the wind dropped. But Bedingfield had been ordered to bring her to Mary, and he couldn't wait to do so. The party struggled on through wind and rain and arrived soaked to the skin.

Elizabeth had hoped for an early interview with Mary. Instead, she was taken in through a back entrance of the palace and given rooms a long way from everyone else. The queen did not want to see her, she was told. But if she confessed her part in the Wyatt conspiracy and asked for forgiveness, the queen would be good to her. There was no way Elizabeth was going to confess to anything. She declared: "Better for me to lie in prison for the truth than to be abroad and suspected of my prince."

Mary was annoyed that Elizabeth was so obstinate. She sent a message that Elizabeth would see no one and go nowhere until she told the truth. But a few days later, Elizabeth was ordered to put on her best dress. King Philip wanted to see her.

No one knows what happened at that meeting, but it seems likely that Philip took a fancy to his wife's sister. She was younger, more attractive, and more of a flirt than Mary. If her later behavior is anything to go by, she was quite capable of encouraging him to think he had a chance if ever he found himself a free man.

Like Philip himself, Elizabeth was a political animal. (Mary's politics always came second to her faith. Sometimes they came third, after her love for her husband.) Both Philip and Elizabeth knew that if Mary were to die in childbirth, they would be the two key players in the land.

After the meeting, Elizabeth went back to her out of the way apartments. She had to wait another two weeks, during which rumors spread around London that Mary had been delivered of a healthy boy. Bonfires were lit, and messengers sent out all over Europe. It was a false alarm. Then, at end of May, came a late-night summons from the queen. Elizabeth was to come and see her at once. Very nervous, Elizabeth was led by torchlight through the dark garden to the queen's private quarters and up to Mary's bedroom by the back stairs.

Perhaps it was Philip who had finally persuaded Mary to see her sister. It is said he was hiding behind a tapestry, listening to the interview that followed. As far as Elizabeth was concerned, she was alone with Mary and one of her ladies-in-waiting in the dark, candlelit bedroom. Elizabeth fell to her knees as all subjects did before their queen and swore, tearfully, that she was Mary's loyal subject.

"In that case," said Mary, "belike you would say that you have been wrongly punished."

"I must not say so, if it please Your Majesty, to you."

"Belike you will say so to others."

"No, if it please Your Majesty. I have borne the burden and I must bear it. I humbly beseech Your Majesty to have a good opinion of me, and to think me to be your true subject, not only from the beginning but for ever, as long as life lasteth."

"Who knows?" said Mary, grumpily, in Spanish, turning toward the tapestry.

The interview over, Elizabeth was shown out. Gradually, it became clear that her house arrest was at an end. Rumor had it that she was under Philip's protection, even that he planned to marry her if Mary died. In 1557, the Venetian ambassador wrote:

> At the time of the Queen's pregnancy the Lady Elizabeth contrived to ingratiate herself with all the Spaniards, and especially with the King, as ever since no one has favored her more than he does....

This did not mean that Elizabeth was having an easy time. She might have been back at court, but people were afraid to speak to her. It was now a burning offense to be a heretic, and so, more than ever, Elizabeth had to play by Mary's rules. She went to mass every day with the king and queen. And like everyone else, she waited for Mary's child to be born. Like Mary, she knew that Mary could die or the child could be born dead. But if Mary died and the child lived, then Elizabeth would be pushed aside and England would have an infant for its sovereign. It must have been hard for Elizabeth to wish her sister and her unborn baby well.

Mary
The Jealous Wife
1555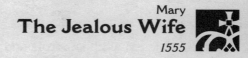

FOR MARY IT MUST have been unbearable to see Philip taken in by — and taken with — Elizabeth. It must have stirred all her adolescent memories. Was there nothing her sister wouldn't take from her, given half the chance?

Mary clung to the hope that the child she was about to produce would solve all her problems. But what nobody knew at the time — although Philip may have guessed — was that Mary was not pregnant at all. Certainly, there was gossip around the court. The Venetian ambassador thought she was too thin and she wasn't eating enough for a woman so far advanced in pregnancy. But there were no ultrasound scans in those days, and Mary had a big belly, so when the baby did not appear when it was due in May, most people thought she had gotten her dates wrong.

June passed, then July. Still there was no baby. Mary sat on the floor for hours on end with her knees drawn up to her chest against the pain. That in itself made other people sure that whatever was causing the pain, it was not a baby. Nevertheless, Mary still insisted she was pregnant.

Finally, in August, all the doctors and midwives and wet nurses were sent away. The cradle was removed from the queen's bedroom. Without any definite announcement, it was understood that the queen was no longer pregnant. No one knows quite what had happened, but it is possible that she wanted a baby so much that she suffered a phantom pregnancy, where the body produces all the signs of pregnancy except for the child itself.

Behind her back, Mary was now a laughingstock. Worst of all, Philip had had enough. For months he had wanted to leave the country to go and fight the French. The only thing keeping him in England had been the imminent birth of an English heir. Now that that was not to be, he was sick of his doting wife and made plans to leave immediately. To reassure Mary, he lied and said he would be back within a few weeks.

Mary took his departure badly. She sat weeping and gazing at the river for hours and days after he had gone. Then she turned to fasting and religious services. Elizabeth was at her side, going through the motions of sharing the same faith as Mary. She even fasted for three days to obtain the pope's forgiveness for her sins and to ask blessings on Philip's campaign.

Before he left, Philip had told Mary that she was to show Elizabeth the respect that was due to the heir to the throne. Mary agreed, though she clearly didn't want to spend much time with Elizabeth. Six weeks after Philip's departure, she allowed her sister to return to her own estate at Hatfield.

Did she hope that, left to her own devices, Elizabeth would become involved in fresh plots? If so, she wouldn't have long to wait.

Elizabeth
Protected Princess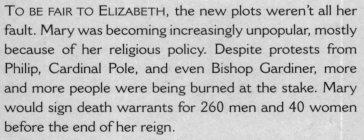
1556

TO BE FAIR TO ELIZABETH, the new plots weren't all her fault. Mary was becoming increasingly unpopular, mostly because of her religious policy. Despite protests from Philip, Cardinal Pole, and even Bishop Gardiner, more and more people were being burned at the stake. Mary would sign death warrants for 260 men and 40 women before the end of her reign.

This and other policies, such as trying to restore the lands confiscated from the Church in Henry's time, put a lot of people against Mary. Elizabeth was probably not the prime mover in any of the attempted rebellions, but she had been sidelined in the past when Northumberland and Suffolk had tried to put Jane Grey on the throne. If a Protestant rebellion were to succeed, Elizabeth must have wanted to be sure it didn't happen without her.

In fact, the next rebellion failed just as surely as Wyatt's. It was led by Sir Anthony Kingston. He was a member of Parliament from Gloucestershire, and very angry. To return land and revenue to the Catholic Church that Henry VIII had taken for himself, Mary needed Parliament to agree to a bill. The members of Parliament were not keen on this. They were even less enthusiastic about another bill which said that the property of Protestant exiles would go to the crown. Kingston locked the members in and Mary's ministers out while he spoke passionately against the bill. Many of the members of Parliament were from families whose fortunes would be affected by it. The bill was defeated, but when the doors were opened, Kingston was marched off to the Tower.

In order to get out, Kingston was forced to apologize, but now he was angrier than ever. He swore that no one would ever treat him like that again. He and others began organizing a fresh rebellion. Like Wyatt before them, their idea was to put Elizabeth and Edward Courtenay jointly on the throne.

The plotters were not very discreet, and Mary's agents had no difficulty keeping track of their plans. They knew that many of Elizabeth's servants and several of her admirers were involved. And so, on May 26, 1556, a troop of armed men once again arrived at Hatfield House. The place was searched, as was Elizabeth's London house. Protestant pamphlets and cartoons of Mary and Philip that were supposed to belong to Kat

Ashley were found. Once again, it looked bad for Elizabeth.

Elizabeth's servants were arrested and taken away. Elizabeth herself was kept under house arrest at Hatfield while Mary sent a message to Philip, asking what should be done with her. Perhaps she hoped that now Philip would believe her about how untrustworthy Elizabeth was. Perhaps he did. But whatever he believed, he did not want Elizabeth tried or imprisoned. Above all, he did not want her executed. For Philip probably guessed that his wife would not live long. And if Mary died, he wanted Elizabeth to become queen of England.

The reason was simple. The alternative to Elizabeth was the Catholic Mary Queen of Scots, cousin to Elizabeth and Mary, and another granddaughter of Henry VII. Mary Queen of Scots was now 14. She had been betrothed to the son of the king of France since she was a baby and would soon be old enough to marry him. And the French king was still Philip's archenemy. If Mary Queen of Scots succeeded to the throne of England, then the French would control the whole of the island of Britain. For Philip, this was far more important than whether Elizabeth was a danger to his wife. It must not be allowed to happen.

Philip sent a message back to Mary telling her not to arrest Elizabeth. As a result, charges had to be dropped against other plotters, too, in case the whole thing unraveled. A couple of minor players were executed, others fled to Europe, and Kat Ashley, who was always getting Elizabeth into trouble — or perhaps taking the blame for the trouble Elizabeth caused herself— was put in prison.

Mary let Elizabeth know how much she knew. She told her what her servants had admitted but pretended that she thought Elizabeth wasn't involved. She invited her to come to court to apologize for her servants' behavior. Elizabeth declined. She now knew beyond doubt that she had Philip's protection. Mary could whistle to the wind.

Abandoned Wife

1556 – 1557

MARY WAS GETTING fed up with Philip, and not only because he was protecting Elizabeth. Her main complaint against him was that he was never home. How could she achieve the one thing she longed for — a baby — when Philip stayed abroad so much of the time? She appealed to his father to send Philip home to her. As usual, Charles took little notice. He had a lot to think about, and Mary was way down his list of priorities. Besides, Philip may have told him what a pain he found Mary.

Mary's tone became angrier, and she wrote to Charles:

> *It would be pleasanter for me to be able to thank Your Majesty for sending me back the King, my lord and good husband... than to despatch an emissary to Flanders.*

However, as Your Majesty has been pleased to break your promise in this connection, a promise you made to me regarding the return of the King my husband, I must perforce be satisfied, although to my unspeakable regret....

Soon she was reported to be so angry at what she saw as Philip's endless excuses that she took down his portrait from the wall and kicked it out of the room, in full view of some of her councillors.

The problem was the very one that Mary's father and so many other Englishmen had foreseen. It was all very well to have the queen of England marry a powerful husband, but the more powerful he was, the less important England would be to him.

There was always going to be a lot going on in Philip's other territories. The Hapsburgs had been at war with France and her allies on and off for 30 years. From that flowed many other things. For instance, in 1555 Philip tried, unsuccessfully, to prevent one of his father's old enemies from becoming pope. Paul IV was a fierce old man of 80 when he was elected pope. He hated Philip's family because as a boy he had seen what the troops of Ferdinand of Aragon (Mary's maternal grandfather) had done to his home city of Naples and its people. Later, he had seen Charles V take Milan and Rome and hold the pope prisoner, way back in the years when Henry VIII had wanted his divorce from Catherine of Aragon. When he discovered that Philip had plotted against his election as pope, his fury knew no bounds.

Once again, the war between France and the Holy Roman Empire was being fought in Italy. Philip, now king of Spain, following the abdication of his father in January 1556, sent an army to besiege Rome, the city where the pope lived. Because of the ferocity of the previous invasion, the people were so frightened that even monks and nuns came out into the streets to dig defenses. And the pope excommunicated Philip. This created an interesting situation for Mary. She was doing her level best to bring England back into the bosom of Catholicism, and now she found herself married to a heretic.

Things became even more interesting later in the year. For there was one reason, and one reason only, that might bring Philip to court Mary again: money. War was expensive, and Philip's coffers were emptying fast. Philip needed fresh funds and fresh fighting men for his war.

So as 1556 wore on, Mary suddenly started receiving frequent letters from Philip, asking for her support. Mary, hopelessly dependent on her husband, assumed he cared about her and that if she helped him enough he would care even more. She sent him intelligence (from English spies in France); she borrowed money for him; she promised him the support of the English navy. She wrote to the sheriffs of nearby towns, asking how many armed men they could supply. In January 1557, she inspected a gathering of troops at Greenwich. The men were all dressed in the Tudor colors of green and white, carrying new flags that combined the white hart of England (a deer) and the black eagle of the Hapsburgs.

Mary's Council was appalled at these arrangements, and the French ambassador thought she was crazy. He wrote:

> She is on the eve of bankrupting either her own mind or her own kingdom. . . . It is impossible that the crown will not fall from her head and roll so far that someone else may pick it up before she has wept for her sins.

At this point, Mary wanted only one thing — the return of her husband. And in March 1557, she got her wish. Philip arrived in England. Mary must have had quite a shock when she saw him, for Philip had aged in the 18 months he had been away. He had spent most of his time hunched over state papers. He had put on weight, his body was bent, and his faced was lined with worry.

Mary had laid on all sorts of celebrations in honor of his return, but Philip was there on business. He hadn't been home a week before he told Mary that unless she got her Council to declare war on the French, she would never see him again. Mary then proceeded to lean very hard on her Council. She threatened them individually, telling them she would take their lands or even have them executed if they did not support Philip. In the end, they all agreed, and on June 7, 1557, England declared war on France. When the king of France was told, he sent a message back that was patronizing but accurate, saying that he knew Mary was only doing it to please her husband.

Philip had not been faithful to Mary while he'd been away. When he arrived in England, he brought with him the Duchess of Parma and the Duchess of Lorraine. There were many rumors about why, but the one that upset Mary was that the Duchess of Lorraine was Philip's new girlfriend. She made sure that the Duchess was housed in apartments as far from Philip's as possible, but that didn't stop them from getting together. By June, Mary was so angry that she ordered the Duchess to pack her bags and get out.

Philip stayed in England for a few more weeks. He was not there for Mary. He was waiting until his old friend, Ruy Gomez, arrived with money and the promise of more fighting men from Spain. The following month, Philip left England. And as soon as he was gone, Mary was once again convinced she was pregnant.

It was the one bit of good news for Mary. Otherwise, the news was dire. England was in the middle of a drought. The crops were failing and her people were starving. And, the final humiliation, the French had captured Calais. It was the last remaining English stronghold in France, and now it was gone forever.

In supporting her husband, Mary was not serving

England's interests. In fact, all in all, Mary was proving to be a disastrous queen.

Elizabeth
Her Turn Next
1556 – 1558

IT MUST HAVE AMUSED Elizabeth when Philip was excommunicated by the pope. Finally, Mary was getting a taste of what their father had been up against: the pope as an ally of the enemy. However, it was not funny when Mary sent men and money to support Philip's endless war with France. Elizabeth would never have done such a thing.

On Mary's orders, Elizabeth had been kept a prisoner in her own house since the failed Kingston rebellion. Then, toward the end of 1556, it seemed that Elizabeth was forgiven. Her house arrest was lifted, and Mary invited her to come to court for the Christmas season.

What Elizabeth did not know as she rode out surrounded by her lords and ladies, all dressed in her livery (colors), was that Philip had plans for her. He wanted her to marry a great friend of his, Emmanuel

Philibert, Duke of Savoy. A marriage to the heiress presumptive of the throne of England would be a fine reward for the Duke. It would also mean that if and when Elizabeth became queen, Philip would have control of her through his ally.

When Elizabeth was told of Philip's proposal, she was horrified. She refused even to consider marrying the Duke of Savoy. Mary told her that in that case she would get Parliament to pass an act confirming she was illegitimate and naming Mary Queen of Scots as heir to the throne of England. Elizabeth was sent home in disgrace before the Christmas celebrations. Worst and most frightening of all, Elizabeth found herself at odds with Philip. It meant that she was without her protector.

Elizabeth was so alarmed that she thought she might have to flee the country. She sent the Countess of Sussex to seek help. The Countess was an old friend of Catherine Parr's, a colorful character who had left her husband over their religious differences and spent time in the Tower for witchcraft. She went in disguise to see the French ambassador on Elizabeth's behalf. The ambassador thought it was unwise for Elizabeth to leave the country, and said so. If anything were to happen to Mary, then Elizabeth needed to be in England to claim her rights.

So Elizabeth stayed. And Philip continued to press Mary to get her to marry the Duke of Savoy. When Philip arrived in England to get money and men for his war with France, the pressure increased. One day, Lady

Northampton came to Elizabeth with a message from the French ambassador. The real reason why the Duchesses of Lorraine and Parma had come to England was, said the ambassador, because they planned to kidnap Elizabeth, take her to Europe, and forcibly marry her to the Duke of Savoy.

Elizabeth was horrified. She sent Lady Northampton back with a message that she would rather die first. She meant it. Elizabeth had never been prepared to die for her faith, but she was ready to fight for her royal rights. No one forced a princess to marry. And if she became queen of England, it would be because it was due to her under her father's will and Act of Parliament, not because the king of Spain had struck a bargain with his wife and an ally.

Curiously, Mary was coming around to Elizabeth's way of thinking, though for completely different reasons. When Philip had first suggested the marriage, she had thought it a good idea — perhaps because of the rumors that Philip planned to marry Elizabeth after she was gone. If Elizabeth was married to someone else, at least she couldn't have Philip. But then Mary began to think about the implications a bit more carefully. Like Elizabeth, she realized that this was all part of a deal. Philip would support Elizabeth's succession to the throne, provided she was married to one of his loyal supporters.

Mary did not like that. Privately, her intention was that Elizabeth should never be queen. She had always hoped that the birth of her own child would put an end to her half sister's chances. If not, she was quite prepared to name someone else as her successor.

Elizabeth was under no illusions about this. She also knew that, for the moment, she needed Mary as an ally against Philip. And so she went through the motions of being friendly with Mary. It must have been difficult. Not only was Mary making a complete mess of running the country, but the burnings had killed some of Elizabeth's personal friends. Archbishop Cranmer, who had been a friend to Elizabeth's mother, who had baptized her, and whose prayer book she loved to use, had been excommunicated by the new pope, Paul IV. As a result, Cranmer had been handed over to the civil authorities to be burned at the stake.

As Elizabeth herself might have done, he had recanted (renounced) his "wrong" beliefs, thinking it might save his life. He was mistaken. He was told he would be burned anyway, and he was taken to a church in Oxford that was packed with people waiting to hear him repeat his recantation. Instead, he spoke up for his Protestant faith. He said that he would thrust his recantation, and the hand that had written it, first into the flames. He spoke until he was shouted down by the crowd that had come to hear him recant. Then, having spoken what he truly believed, he was led away to his execution.

Like many others, he died bravely. Mary's policy was not deterring heretics. Instead, it was creating martyrs and strengthening the Protestant cause. In 1557, a Register of Martyrs was printed on a secret press. Each list of martyrs ended with a rhyme:

WHEN THESE WITH VIOLENCE WERE BURNED TO DEATH
WE WISHED FOR OUR ELIZABETH.

Both Elizabeth and Mary must have known of this. Nevertheless, they continued to play their roles as friendly sisters. Elizabeth went on pretending to be a devout Catholic. Mary paid her a friendly visit at Hatfield. And in February 1558, Elizabeth went to stay with Mary, bringing with her a layette of baby clothes she had made herself.

One of the things we know about Elizabeth at this time is that she was short of money. Not because she did not have a big enough income but because her income had to go a very long way. All the liveries her people rode out in cost money. And according to one modern historian, David Starkey, she was spending on what was effectively a political campaign. She was making sure that up and down the country she could count on the support of various noblemen and landowners when the time came.

Like Philip, Elizabeth had guessed that Mary's continuing stomach pains meant she was ill. And she knew that under Henry's will, it was her turn next. But she also knew that she might have to fight for her kingdom.

Mary
Prey to the Hatred
1558

AT THE BEGINNING OF 1558, Philip urged Mary to make a will naming Elizabeth as her heir. This was the last thing Mary wanted to do. Mary now made no secret of the fact that, in her opinion, Elizabeth had "the face and countenance of Mark Smeaton." (He was a court musician who had been one of the men executed for adultery along with Anne Boleyn.) It suited Mary for Elizabeth to be Smeaton's child, not Henry's, for then Elizabeth had absolutely no right to the throne of England.

Mary still clung to the idea that she was pregnant, even though it was now nine months since Philip had left and most people thought her belly was not nearly big enough for her to be carrying a baby. So, when in March of that year she did make a will, she left her crown to "the heirs, issue and fruit of my body." She also left money for the reburial of her mother in Westminster

Abbey and to the new abbeys and monasteries she had founded. She instructed Cardinal Pole to carry on giving back money that her father had taken from the Church, and she commanded her subjects to obey Philip.

Every instruction in the will showed what a fantasy world Mary was living in. She was not pregnant. If she had wanted to rebury her mother, Mary could have done it herself. Pole was on his deathbed, and in any case, her policy of restoring Catholicism had proved a hopeless failure. Her subjects hated Philip with a passion and had done so since before she married him. There was absolutely no chance they would treat him as their king after she was gone.

By this time, no one had a good word to say about Mary, except a few personal friends and servants. A former minister in her brother's government wrote about the end of her reign:

> I never saw England weaker in strength, money, men and riches. As much affectionate as you know me to be to my country and countrymen, I assure you I was ashamed of them both. Here was nothing but fining, heading, hanging, quartering, and burning, taxing, levying and beggaring, and losing our strongholds abroad. A few priests ruled all, who, with setting up of six foot roods [crucifixes], thought to make all cocksure.

No wonder that in 1557 a cartoon was going the rounds mocking Mary and calling her "England's Ruin."

In April 1558, Mary realized that she wasn't pregnant, after all. From then on she seems to have sunk into a terrible depression, spending days on end in "a death-like stupor." Michieli, the Venetian ambassador, wrote very insightfully at the time about its causes. It was due, he said, to her childlessness, to the fact that her husband didn't love her, to her debts, to fact she had become a laughingstock, to the plots against her life. But the thing that annoyed her most of all, according to Michieli, was that:

> She is prey to the hatred she bears my Lady Elizabeth... [both because of]... the recollection of the wrongs she experienced on account of her mother... [and also]... to see the illegitimate child of a criminal who was punished as a public strumpet on the point of inheriting the throne with better fortune than herself, whose descent is rightful, legitimate and regal.

In other words, she was eaten up with resentment and hated the fact that Elizabeth, the daughter of the woman who had supplanted her mother, was going to succeed her.

All this was made worse by the fact that, even though Elizabeth had turned down the Duke of Savoy, Philip still supported her claim to the throne. The reason was simple. He still needed England as an ally. He sent the Duke of Feria over to England, supposedly to see how Mary's health was, but really to test the waters on his behalf with Elizabeth. Philip wanted her as, at the very least, an ally. He was also hoping that when Mary died, she might become his wife.

By the time the Duke arrived, Mary seems to have decided that there was no other choice but Elizabeth. Her lady-in-waiting Jane Dormer arrived at Hatfield with a message from Mary. She would name Elizabeth as heir to the throne on two conditions: one, that Elizabeth would pay off Mary's debts, and two, that she would keep the Catholic religion as the established religion of England. Perhaps Mary was doing as her father had once done to her, and trying to trap Elizabeth, getting her to reveal that she was not a true Catholic. If it was a trap, Elizabeth deftly avoided it. According to Jane, Elizabeth "prayed to God that the earth might open and swallow her alive if she were not a true Roman Catholic."

Meanwhile, in case his wife did not die, Philip was still sending Mary letters urging her to get Elizabeth married to the Duke of Savoy. Mary never read them; she was now unconscious most of the time. It was reported that sometimes, when she woke:

> ... she told them what good dreams she had, seeing many little children like angels playing before her, singing pleasing notes, giving her more than earthly comfort.

Right up to the eve of her death, Mary insisted on hearing mass when she was conscious. Then, after making her last confession on November 17, 1558, she slipped quietly from sleep into death.

Elizabeth
"This Is the Lord's Doing"
1558

LEGEND HAS IT THAT Elizabeth was sitting under an oak tree at Hatfield, reading a book, when the Privy Councillors arrived to tell her she was queen. She is supposed to have said, "This is the Lord's doing, and marvellous in our eyes." The story makes her sound like a starry-eyed young girl, taken by surprise by the news.

In fact, of course, Elizabeth had known for weeks that her sister was dying. And she had been preparing for the moment for years. She would have been foolish not to have done so. There were plenty of other people willing to claim the throne, and plenty more ready to say she was illegitimate and had no right to it.

Elizabeth was to become one of the shrewdest rulers that England had ever seen. She could hold her own with every monarch in Europe. And that political ability didn't drop out of the sky on her with the news that she was queen. Quietly, in secret, for it was treason to do so before her sister was dead, she and her people had been making preparations. Already William Cecil knew he was to be her secretary of state. Other people also knew what jobs they were to do and were perhaps already doing them. There were probably also arrangements in place in case anyone decided she shouldn't be queen — arms, men, money at the ready. As it happened, they were not needed. For the first time in 130 years, one monarch succeeded another peacefully.

Now Elizabeth was able to be her own person. She no longer had to live in fear of putting a foot wrong. She could flirt if she wanted — and she did. She no longer had to pretend to believe things she didn't believe. She could wear what she wanted. No more black-and-white clothes for her now. She wore the sumptuous colors encrusted with jewels that she loved. Now neither Philip nor anyone else could make her marry. She was queen!

But Elizabeth had spent a long time on the sidelines. She had watched her father, then her brother, and finally her sister in action. From their mistakes she had learned a lot of lessons.

From Henry, Elizabeth had learned the value of strength, pageant, and majesty. She had also learned that war bankrupted the country and that even kings became unpopular when they were hypocritical about their motives. From Edward and his Council, she'd decided she didn't like extreme Protestants.

From Mary, she'd learned most of all, because Mary was a woman. Elizabeth had the good fortune to watch her sister fall into the traps that had beset many women rulers since the dawn of history. She'd seen how dangerous marriage was for a queen, for if she married a foreign prince she would be towed into his wars and conflicts, and if she married one of her own subjects the others would be jealous and gang up on her. She'd seen how love had made Mary blind to Philip's motives and how her pregnancies, even though they had been imaginary, had removed her from government for months. She knew firsthand how Philip had been prepared to strike a deal with her when he thought Mary might die in childbirth.

Elizabeth had learned that a monarch could never know what was going on inside his or her subjects' heads when it came to religious belief. She'd also learned that persecution made enemies and made people hate their monarch and their religion. She'd learned it was a mistake to go head-to-head with Parliament. Better to back off and try again later.

Elizabeth may even have learned to like aspects of Catholicism from the time Mary forced her to go to Catholic mass. Although she would never believe in the authority of the pope, Elizabeth enjoyed a very un-Protestant love of ritual and sacred music. She restored some of the beautiful old abbeys that had fallen into disrepair, and they became places of worship again under the Church of England.

Above all, she knew that as heir to the throne, she had been a magnet for people who didn't like Queen Mary, whether she encouraged them or not. That was why she would never name her successor.

Elizabeth put all those lessons and more into ruling England, but that, of course, is another story. Suffice it to say that, although she fell in love more than once, she never married. She kept Philip, and many other suitors down the years, guessing. She realized that the prospect of marriage to the queen of England was her strongest card, which would lose its value if ever she played it. She never commented on her father's policies or on what he had done to her mother. She paid off Mary's debts as she had promised, but she did not restore the Catholic Church to England. She cultivated the arts and patronized many musicians and artists, Catholic and Protestant alike. She invested in the voyages of her seafarers and pocketed a share of their pirated gains. Although she flirted till the end of her life, Elizabeth ran a strict court, looking after the morals and welfare of her ladies-in-waiting. In 1588, her sailors won a great battle against the Spanish, and for the rest of her reign she was known as Gloriana. The Elizabethan Age is famous to this day for the greatness of England under Elizabeth.

Afterword

ALL IN ALL, it's not very difficult to see why Elizabeth and Mary were poles apart. Although they had the same father, they were brought up completely differently. Mary was the princess royal until she was 18 and Elizabeth supplanted her. Elizabeth was demoted before she was three. This meant that Mary had high expectations, while Elizabeth knew, almost from birth, that her position was precarious.

In addition, Mary was of royal blood on her mother's side and came from one of the most powerful families in Europe. Elizabeth had only her mother's English friends and family on her side, and many of them weren't very reliable.

Mary married a foreigner, and as a result England was towed into a foreign war that the nation could not afford. Elizabeth had the sense to realize that her power lay in *not* marrying. That way, hopeful foreign suitors would do what she wanted.

Above all, Mary was not just a passionate Catholic, but a Catholic with an agenda. She wanted to see England a Catholic country again as it had been in her youth. This was far more important to her than governing England well. Elizabeth, on the other hand, always put England first. Whatever she felt privately, she was prepared to be tolerant. It was only after religious beliefs caused people to plot against her that she became hostile to Catholics.

Did the sisters like each other? Almost certainly not. Their mothers had been enemies, and Elizabeth's birth upset all the certainties of Mary's world. For Elizabeth, Mary was an angry, threatening grown-up from the start. The moments when they were friends were few and far between.

The fact was that neither could ever forget how much there was at stake. From the moment of Elizabeth's birth until the day of Mary's death, these sisters were rivals for the crown.

Family Tree of Mary and Elizabeth

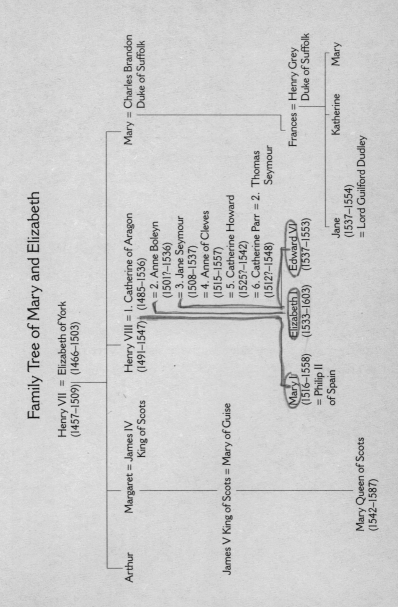

Henry VII = Elizabeth of York
(1457–1509)   (1466–1503)

Arthur

Margaret = James IV
King of Scots

James V King of Scots = Mary of Guise

Mary Queen of Scots
(1542–1587)

Henry VIII = 1. Catherine of Aragon
(1491–1547)   (1485–1536)
= 2. Anne Boleyn
(1501?–1536)
= 3. Jane Seymour
(1508–1537)
= 4. Anne of Cleves
(1515–1557)
= 5. Catherine Howard
(1525?–1542)
= 6. Catherine Parr = 2. Thomas
(1512?–1548)   Seymour

Mary I
(1516–1558)
= Philip II
of Spain

Elizabeth I
(1533–1603)

Edward VI
(1537–1553)

Mary = Charles Brandon
          Duke of Suffolk

Frances = Henry Grey
               Duke of Suffolk

Jane
(1537–1554)
= Lord Guilford Dudley

Katherine

Mary

Further Reading

The Life and Times of Henry VIII by Robert Lacey (Weidenfeld and Nicholson, 1972)

Children of England by Alison Weir (Jonathan Cape, 1997)

Elizabeth by David Starkey (Chatto and Windus, 2000)

Bloody Mary by Carolly Erickson (Robson Books, 2001)

The Six Wives of Henry VIII by Antonia Fraser (Weidenfeld and Nicholson, 1992)

Index